# IRENA'S CHILDREN

ALSO BY TILAR J. MAZZEO

*The Widow Clicquot:*
*The Story of a Champagne Empire and the Woman Who Ruled It*

*The Secret of Chanel No. 5:*
*The Intimate History of the World's Most Famous Perfume*

*The Hotel on Place Vendôme:*
*Life, Death, and Betrayal at the Hôtel Ritz in Paris*

ALSO BY MARY CRONK FARRELL

*Pure Grit: How American World War II Nurses Survived*
*Battle and Prison Camp in the Pacific*

# IRENA'S CHILDREN

## YOUNG READERS EDITION

A true story of courage by

*Tilar J. Mazzeo*

Adapted by

*Mary Cronk Farrell*

MARGARET K. McELDERRY BOOKS

New York   London   Toronto   Sydney   New Delhi

MARGARET K. McELDERRY BOOKS
An imprint of Simon & Schuster Children's Publishing Division
1230 Avenue of the Americas, New York, New York 10020
The views or opinions expressed in this book, and the context in which the images are used, do not necessarily reflect the views or policy of, nor imply approval or endorsement by, the United States Holocaust Memorial Museum, Yad Vashem, or any other content licensor.
Text copyright © 2016 by Tilar Mazzeo
Young Readers Edition adaptation copyright © 2016 by Tilar Mazzeo
Illustrations copyright © 2016 by Shana Torok
Hand-lettering by Shana Torok
All rights reserved, including the right of reproduction in whole or in part in any form.
MARGARET K. McELDERRY BOOKS is a trademark of Simon & Schuster, Inc. For information about special discounts for bulk purchases, please contact Simon & Schuster Special Sales at 1-866-506-1949 or business@simonandschuster.com.
The Simon & Schuster Speakers Bureau can bring authors to your live event. For more information or to book an event, contact the Simon & Schuster Speakers Bureau at 1-866-248-3049 or visit our website at www.simonspeakers.com.
Also available in a Margaret K. McElderry Books hardcover edition
Book design by Lauren Rille
The text for this book was set in Adobe Garamond Pro.
Manufactured in the United States of America
1219 OFF
First Margaret K. McElderry Books paperback edition September 2017
10  9  8  7  6  5  4
The Library of Congress has cataloged the hardcover edition as follows:
Names: Mazzeo, Tilar J., author. | Farrell, Mary Cronk, author. | Torok, Shana, illustrator.
Title: Irena's children : a true story of courage by Tilar J. Mazzeo / adapted by Mary Cronk Farrell.
Description: Young readers edition. | New York : Margaret K. McElderry Books, [2016] | Includes bibliographical references and index.
Identifiers: LCCN 2016004169 (print) | LCCN 2015051244 (eBook) |
ISBN 9781481449915 (hardcover : alk. paper) | ISBN 9781481449922 (pbk. : alk. paper) | ISBN 9781481449939 (eBook) | ISBN 9781476778501 (hardcover : alk. paper) | ISBN 9781476778518 (pbk. : alk. paper) | ISBN 9781476778525 (eBook)
Subjects: LCSH: Sendlerowa, Irena, 1910–2008—Juvenile literature. | Righteous Gentiles in the Holocaust—Poland—Biography—Juvenile literature. | World War, 1939–1945—Jews—Rescue—Poland—Juvenile literature. | Holocaust, Jewish (1939–1945)—Poland—Juvenile literature. | Jewish children in the Holocaust—Poland—Warsaw—Juvenile literature. | Jews—Poland—Warsaw—History—20th century—Juvenile literature. | World War, 1939–1945—Poland—Warsaw—Juvenile literature. | Warsaw (Poland)—Biography—Juvenile literature.
Classification: LCC D804.34 .M39 2016+ (print) | LCC D804.66.S46 M29 2016 (eBook) | DDC 940.53/18092—dc23
LC record available at http://lccn.loc.gov/2016004169

For Addie and Xavi, Eddie and Rory,
who would always be brave

# Contents

## Introduction

In her native Poland, Irena Sendler is a famous heroine today. But it took a long time for her to become famous. Her story, like so many stories across Poland, was quietly buried for decades. The Soviets, who occupied Poland after the end of the Second World War, didn't want people to tell each other stories about the bravery and courage of people who had fought to make Poland independent. It might encourage other Polish people to want to fight again for their freedom. In the 1980s, things finally started to change in Poland, and there was a new movement known as Solidarność—"solidarity." As Solidarność took hold of people's imaginations across the world, things happened so quickly many couldn't believe the changes. Eventually, thanks to "solidarity" and changes around the world, even the Berlin Wall, which kept people in the east apart from people in the west, was dismantled while crowds from around the globe cheered. The Soviet Union also disappeared as a country. And suddenly, for the first time in decades, it was safe to tell some of the stories of brave and amazing people in Poland like Irena Sendler and her friends, who risked their lives during the Second World War to help save Jewish families and, especially, Jewish children and teenagers.

With her friends, Irena Sendler smuggled infants out of the Warsaw ghetto, past German guards and Jewish police traitors, in suitcases and wooden boxes. She carried toddlers and school children through the city's foul and dangerous sewers. Some of the kids hid underneath the corpses of dead bodies in coffins in order to get past the guards—people history calls the Nazis—who wanted to kill them. She worked with Jewish teenagers—many of them astonishingly brave girls and boys of fourteen or fifteen—who helped her smuggle little children out of the ghetto. Many also later fought and died in the ghetto uprising. And, through it all, she and her friends spent the war hiding and taking care of thousands of children.

Irena was a small person, but she had a gigantic heart. She was a four-foot-eleven-inch tall wisp of a young woman, in her late twenties when the war began, and she didn't have any experience in battles or in fighting. But faced with a situation she knew was wrong, Irena was determined to stand up to bullying and to take action to do what she believed in, and she learned quickly. Irena fought with all her ferocity and intelligence. Soon she was acting like an experienced general. Her foot soldiers and her army were dozens of ordinary people, across the city of Warsaw, who agreed to help hide children from the Nazis and to save them.

Before she was arrested and threatened with execution for her actions, Irena Sendler and her friends saved the lives of more than two thousand Jewish children. At immense risk she also did something ever more courageous. Irena and her friends kept a list of the children's names so that after the war their parents could find them. Many of the children's parents did not survive the war and died in the great killings of the Holocaust. But thousands of Irena's children survived, and many of them went on to become mothers and fathers. None of them ever forgot the bravery of the woman who helped save them.

But, while Irena Sendler was undeniably a heroine—a woman of immense, almost unimaginable courage—she hated being called a hero. "Heroes," she said, "do extraordinary things. What I did was not an extraordinary thing. It was normal." It should have been normal, is what Irena meant when she said that. If everyone had dared to stand up for what was right, something terrible might not have happened.

Not everyone in Poland had the courage to stand up to the Nazis. Most people weren't brave. But Irena wasn't alone either. Dozens of people quietly joined her. Irena said that for each child whose rescue she organized, ten people in Warsaw risked their lives to help in the mission. For those who helped Irena, the choices were monstrous. Punishment for helping a Jew meant having your whole family killed in front of you. Yet not once did any of these people—dozens of them—flinch from helping Irena in her mission. No one, Irena once said, ever refused to take in one of her children.

This is the story of Irena Sendler, the children she saved, and some of those brave and average people who helped her. If you had been alive during the dark days of the Second World War, would you have been one of the people who joined her? Irena Sendler's story inspires everyone—grown-ups and young people—to ask themselves that important question.

—*Tilar J. Mazzeo*

Poland was a special place for Jewish people. It became home and haven for them in the eleventh through thirteenth centuries when the Christian Crusades threatened them with persecution and death. In the beginning, they were welcome to settle in the towns and villages. Laws gave them legal and professional rights and guarded their freedom to gather and worship as they pleased.

As time went by, the Jewish people prospered, trading in cloth, horses, and cattle, owning land, developing skills with leather and wood, some growing wealthy. Sadly, a pattern of Jewish history began to repeat itself. Some people resented the Jews and their success. Dislike grew to anger and hatred, and when bad things happened, like the plague, people wanted someone to blame. They blamed the Jews, and they did it with a vengeance, massacring men, women, and children throughout the land. Times of peace followed times of violence over and over again. Still, the Jewish people of Poland flourished and multiplied.

Over the centuries, Poland had become the center of Jewish culture in Europe, and the city of Warsaw became the mainspring of Jewish theater, music, architecture, publishing, Judaic scholarship, and social reform. Warsaw Jews made contributions to the world in math, economics, law, and science. By Irena's time, more than 3.3 million Jews lived in Poland, the largest Jewish population in Europe. They lived mostly separate from their more or less tolerant Christian neighbors, but they were a diverse people, having immigrated from all over the continent. Jewish families were poor, rich, and everywhere in between.

But in the 1920s and 1930s, people with strong feelings against Jews gained more power in Poland. In the neighboring country of Germany, the Nazi government took away Jewish people's rights and freedom, making anti-Semitism the law of the land. Once again, for Jews, the best of times turned into the worst of times. In that darkness arose a bright flame that could not be snuffed out.

That beacon burning with moral courage was Irena Sendler. I am delighted and honored to bring her story to life in this edition for young readers. Irena's choice of lifesaving resistance to the power and evil of Nazism proves to me that we humans have great potential to put aside apathy and self-interest, to rise above hatred and fear, and to act with compassion. Knowing Irena's story makes me want to be more fearless and to show more kindness every day. Some parts of the story are so terrible I didn't want to write them, and they might be sad and painful for you to read. But if we don't know about the Nazis' brutality, we can't begin to understand Irena's bravery.

—*Mary Cronk Farrell*

*Irena Sendler*
circa 1942

# Prologue

Young Piotr waited in the shadows. His aunt held his hand and looked down the street, watching the German soldiers. The soldiers did not have to be afraid like everyone else. They had guns swinging at their side. Auntie was holding Piotr's baby cousin in her other arm and the grown-ups were worried. It would be bad if the baby started crying. The soldiers turned the corner at the end of the street. A hand fell heavy on Piotr's shoulder. His father? No. His father was not coming with them, and neither was his mother. He'd never been away from his parents before, and it was hard to understand what was happening. He was four now. *Run!* Someone hissed. *Run!* That's what they were waiting for. Piotr ran. He ran as fast as he could toward the trees where the hole was waiting.

The man helped Piotr and his aunt and his cousin Elżbieta down the dark hole into a tunnel. It smelled *terrible.* It was wet and dark and crowded. "Be quiet," the strange man said to them. "And you must not cry," he told Piotr.

Piotr would not cry. He was not a baby. He followed the man, listening to the unfamiliar noises that echoed from a long way away. Shoes went *squish-squish* in the greasy trickle of water running in the tunnel, and soon his feet were wet. They walked on and on. It was slippery, and it made you tired. But it would be scary to get left behind here. They trudged through the yucky water for a long time.

Sometimes the man stopped so quick that it was hard not to stumble. The man put a finger to his lips. *Quiet.* Then a rattle and distant voices came from above, but the man kept walking and so did Piotr. At last, the man stopped. He pointed. There were rungs of a ladder rising to a grate. After waiting a short time, listening, the man reached up and drew aside the grate, and motioned for them to climb up. They climbed up into the daylight trying not to make any clatter.

Suddenly the man was gone. There to meet them was another stranger, a woman, a small woman. She smiled at him. *Come*, she said. They followed her.

# 1

## War

### September 1, 1939

The wail of sirens dragged Irena from sleep, and she jumped up. Air-raid sirens. An attack? No. Surely, a false alarm.

She and her mother grabbed their bathrobes and slippers. Everywhere, rumpled neighbors were pouring out of their apartment buildings into the street. They peered upward. It was six o'clock in the morning and the low-lying clouds were calm, the streets empty of traffic. The air-raid wardens knew no more than the curious crowd, but shooed everyone back into their buildings. The anxiety and early hour made people cross, and somewhere in the building a door slammed. The sirens continued to wail.

Irena sat with her mother at the kitchen table and turned on Polish radio. Bleary-eyed and grim, they listened to the news. Everyone feared Germany would strike. Irena and her friends had followed news of Adolf Hitler's rise to power in Germany and the antidemocratic policies of his National Socialist German Workers' Party (Nazi party). The German takeover of Czechoslovakia had moved Poland to ready its military for war. But though Irena had known war would come, it was difficult to believe her country—her city—was under attack!

Hovering over the radio, Irena leaned in to hear the words. Government and city workers in the capital were instructed to stay at their posts around the clock, using all efforts to resist the German aggressors. Thank heavens. Irena wanted to do something.

*Irena, stop fidgeting.* A look from her mother told her to sit down and finish her coffee. What could she do anyhow? The minutes ticked by. News trickled in. German armies rolled into Poland from the south, the west, and the north.

By 7:00 a.m. Irena could no longer bear doing nothing, and she flew down the stairs to the courtyard. Tossing her weathered bag into the basket of her bicycle, Irena hitched up her skirt and pedaled quickly toward the Old Town and her office on Zlota Street. It was a relief to be off, to leave the waiting and worrying to her mother. She felt a powerful purpose and determination.

Irena worked as a senior administrator in a branch of the city social welfare office that ran soup kitchens across the city. Reaching her building, she went to look for her boss, Irena—"Irka"—Schultz, a thin, birdlike blonde with a big smile. Irka was more than her supervisor. She was one of Dr. Radlinska's girls, just like Irena was.

While studying at the Polish Free University, Irena had found a warm welcome in Professor Helena Radlinska's circle. The sturdy woman with thinning white hair shared the socialist ideals of Irena's papa, and Irena missed her papa. She'd joined in the radical activism of the tight-knit group of young men and women inspired by Dr. Radlinska. And the professor had given Irena her first social work job at one of her clinics helping the poorest families in Warsaw.

Irena found her boss Irka calm and matter-of-fact, even with the city under siege. For the next few hours, the staff set in motion plans for how they might help families survive this crisis. Irena couldn't imagine what they would face in the coming days. Who knew what war looked like until they were in it? But she knew the families she served would need her help now more than ever.

At about nine o'clock, the women dropped what they were doing. They listened to what sounded like "a faraway surf . . . not a calm surf but when waves crash onto a beach during a storm." Then air-raid sirens pierced their ears, soon joined by a thunder of planes overhead, and Irena heard the first explosions. Bombs. She and the other women ran for cover, while the building rattled with the hum of planes, tens, maybe even hundreds and ear-splitting, ground-shaking concussions. In the cellar bomb shelters, everyone clutched hands in the musty darkness with a faint hope, listening for the Polish defensive artillery firing back.

When the pounding let up and the roar of bombers receded, it was horrible to see how much damage had been done to Warsaw. Irena looked out at a sky black with smoke. Chaos filled Zlota Street. Clouds of dust coated her throat and smoke stung her nose. Some buildings had been turned to rubble. Flames engulfed the gutted facades of entire apartment buildings. The walls swayed and then toppled in a crash to the cobblestones. Piles of bricks lay everywhere, as if thrown by an angry child, and glass and debris littered the ground. Horses fell dead, and Irena saw, there, in the midst of it all, mangled human bodies.

The first onslaught of war was dizzying, unreal. She could not imagine the horrors that were yet to come, and shuddered to think of the soldiers on the front lines, fighting to stop the Germans, the bloodshed they must be facing. A few days ago, she had said good-bye to several men leaving Warsaw for military deployment. A lawyer in the social services office, Jozef Zysman, had been called up as reserve officer, and Irena worried about his wife, Theodora. He was a prominent city attorney, often representing needy people for free. Irena had regularly waited with him in the halls of the courthouse, each of them leaning up against the stair railings and laughing. He defended people illegally evicted from their homes, and Irena was one of his favorite witnesses. She reveled in righting an injustice and could be very persuasive. *She would have to check in on Theodora and their baby.*

Amid the utter confusion, Irena tried to clear her mind. It was her job to provide food in this emergency. People bombed out of their homes would need shelter. She and her coworkers set up dozens of makeshift canteens and shelters. They stood by offering hot soup and blankets.

In the following days the assault was continual, flights of up to fifty bombers, exploding warheads, hitting army barracks, targeting factories, and demolishing apartment buildings, hospitals, and schools. No place was safe from the bombs. It felt especially frightening to go out in the street, but Irena had to check on the soup kitchens she had helped organize. The lines of people waiting for food included families with children of all ages, and grandparents, too.

Many had fled the countryside. They told of running from their homes as the war planes flew over their villages, seeing the bombs demolish their homes. German dive bombers screeched overhead, opening fire on the people, the unarmed, helpless people. Survivors came to Warsaw with little but the clothes they wore. Others, they said, never made it to the city.

Irena moved among the refugees, trying to comfort them. Polish and sometimes Yiddish voices surrounded her, broken with sorrow, high pitched with fear, or low with desperation. With dirty, tearstained faces, villagers recounted how they had joined the throngs of people on the roads, no place to go, but at least not alone.

There was nothing to do, they told Irena, but to keep walking. Her heart seized as she learned of the cruelty of the attacking Germans. But then, the Nazis had turned cruelty and violence against Germany's own people who didn't go along, like socialists, communists, and especially Jewish people. How could one brave an enemy that showed the innocent no mercy? The refugees' plight compelled her to work long days procuring food for the soup kitchens, and investigating the ruins of the city for possible shelters for the homeless.

The Jewish families, their children lined up like stair steps, reminded her of her papa's clinic when she was a child in Otwock. His office had often been filled with the desperate and poor. He had never turned away anyone. When he was tired, he still made rounds in the village. He treated Jewish people when other doctors refused. Her memories of Papa warmed her, for he had doted on her as a child, and in this dark time, his example of compassion became a beacon lighting her way.

Through the week, the intermittent news Irena gleaned from Polish radio did not offer much hope. German tanks and infantry had broken through Polish army defensive lines, scattering whole battalions. Polish forces retreated east in an effort to regroup. On the eighth day of the German attack, Irena learned the enemy now completely surrounded Warsaw.

The news grew worse. On September 17, the Soviet army had invaded Poland's eastern border, and Irena could hear the artillery as the German army breached Warsaw's defenses and poured into the city. She had no choice but to take cover as fighting erupted in the streets and the attacks from the air grew more intense.

Some of Irena's neighbors and coworkers held on to a thread of hope as long as the fighting continued in Warsaw's neighborhoods, but beginning the morning of September 24, the sky over Warsaw darkened with German bombers, hundreds of them—no, it had to be thousands, so many they couldn't be counted. Bombs once again exploded in the city without stopping for hours. A full day. Two days. The floor bumped and rolled with the explosions. Surely, she'd go deaf from the incessant booming and blasting. The brown dust and smothering smoke burned Irena's nose and lungs, stung her eyes.

When the attack finally ended, Irena took stock. From what she could learn, the Germans had clobbered entire districts of Warsaw into ruins. Debris clogged some streets entirely. Whole blocks raged with fire. *Would any of them survive?*

At home, Irena's mother whispered urgent prayers. So did Irena. Still, she put more faith in action and there was more work to do than ever. Some of the worst hit areas of the city included the quarter just north of her office. A mostly Jewish neighborhood, it ran from the Jewish and Polish cemeteries on the west, to the great synagogue on the east. Irena found the homeless had crawled into overcrowded cellars, thick with the smell of gangrene, and too many bodies too close. In the air-raid shelters, the injured lay on stretchers, crying quietly and begging for water.

All the people of Warsaw suffered. There was no water, no electricity, and no longer any food. The air was rank with the smell of human and animal corpses heaped in the streets. Some kind souls buried the dead where they found them, in a garden or a square or the courtyards of houses. Famished people cut flesh from horses as soon as they perished, leaving skeletons in the street.

Irena was at the office trying to fight the chaos by establishing order in her soup kitchens when Polish radio announced the news. The mayor had surrendered the city to the Germans. Everyone in the office was crying and hugging, because it was sad and scary. Out on the street an ominous silence settled over Warsaw, eerie after nearly a month of bombardment.

As the facts became clear, the women in the office tried to comfort one another. Germany and the Soviet Union had struck a deal before the bombing started. The two countries divided Poland like two bullies stealing another boy's marbles and splitting the spoils.

Irena and her friends had a hundred anxious questions. Would the men in the Polish army make it home? And what would they come home to? A smoldering, hungry city burying its dead.

# 2

## *Occupation*

**Warsaw, 1940**

Not long after the bombs stopped falling, Irena realized the Poles faced new terrors. Now, the Nazis controlled Warsaw—the Nazis who believed the Germanic race, people with blond hair and blue eyes, were superior to Polish and especially to Jewish people. Nazi killing squads called the Schutzstaffel Einsatzkommandos, SS for short, marched the streets in their shiny black boots enforcing a dusk to dawn curfew. No one was safe. But Irena was stunned to learn these new rulers were hunting professors at Warsaw's universities, and those found were often straightaway executed. What would happen to her professors at the Polish Free University, dear friends through the years after she'd finished her studies there?

Then staggering news filtered in through friends of friends and relatives. Throughout Poland, the SS was rounding up teachers, priests, landowners, politicians, and journalists, shooting them like animals at slaughter, or deporting them to Germany for slave labor, with only a lucky few managing to hide or flee east to Soviet territory. Everyone wanted to believe all this was false rumor, but it was true. The Nazis were getting rid of anyone with influence, anyone who might lead the Polish people against them, and using terror tactics to scare everyone into submission. Irena, for one, would not be cowed. Irena would find some way to resist the invaders.

But open resistance was fatal. The Nazis shot people for the slightest reasons. Everyone had to apply for German identity cards—*kennkarte*—carry them at all times, and produce them at a moment's notice. These *kennkarte* identified everyone by their religion. Irena's showed that she was Christian.

The Nazis closed schools and burned libraries, kidnapped men, women, and teens off the street and shipped them to labor camps. Thousands of "Aryan-looking" children were stolen from their parents, sent away to be "Germanized" and adopted by German families. Irena and her friends turned to one another to get through this terrible time. She had close friends through her job at the city social work office, and through the Polish Socialist Party. She had gotten her interest in politics from her papa. He had helped found the Polish Socialist Party, way back before Irena was born. She joined the Socialists during her university days, and it was a profound homecoming of sorts, a connection to the papa she still grieved.

All during September, when German bombs had been pounding Warsaw, Irena and her girlfriends, Ala Gołab-Grynberg, Ewa Rechtman, and Rachela Rosenthal, did not feel safe meeting at cafés for coffee or ice cream any longer. Before the war they had dressed fashionably, in low-slung heels and brightly patterned dresses. They were smart, idealistic, bent on changing the world.

Irena loved these friends and the high-spirited good fun they had together. Ewa was the sweet and sensitive one. Ala, on the other hand, was sassy and maybe even a bit intimidating. She was a sharp, angular woman, her clothes never fitting quite properly, her wiry black hair almost always wild and curly. Irena was not in the least vain, but her friends openly displayed their affection for her warmth, and it was a nice compliment that people said they could see the intelligence shining in Irena's blue eyes. Her friends were all from Jewish families, and they howled with laughter to hear Yiddish flowing so freely from the tongue of a girl born Catholic like Irena.

For Irena's part, the Jewish girls reminded her of the magical days of her childhood, when Papa and Mama's home had been open to everyone. Otwock's Jewish families had embraced the doctor's daughter just as her parents had welcomed them. Irena played all her childhood games with the Jewish girls and boys. She spoke a fluent backyard

*Irena's parents, 1903.*

Yiddish by age six and was comforted by the sight of Jewish mothers in their colorful head scarves. She knew that the scent of bread baked with cumin meant something delicious, if the children were lucky.

Now, the Nazis enforced strict order throughout Warsaw and banned all public meetings. Even gathering with a group of friends was dangerous. Irena mostly saw her friends and the men in their circle, Jozef and Adam, at Socialist Party meetings. Even more dangerous! The occupation government had outlawed all political parties except the Nazi party.

Irena and her friends had to meet with other Socialist Party members in back rooms of shops, basements, and behind shaded windows. At first the secret meetings felt exciting, as they whispered code words at the thresholds of dim apartments. *The war will be over soon,* a number of people spoke confidently. *Perhaps until then it will not be so bad under the Germans.* Irena wanted to believe these sentiments, but evidence mounted to the contrary.

Most Poles in Warsaw resisted the brutal occupation forces any way they could. It seemed something of a miracle to Irena, how quickly an organized and determined Polish partisan movement took shape and flourished, led by older men who had not gone off to war, the Jewish community, and a great number of courageous women of all ages, even teenagers.

Dr. Helena Radlinska, a beloved professor at the Polish

Free University, and Irena's mentor in social services work, had taught her that the commitment of a small group of well-intentioned people could shape the world in their vision of it. The time had come to determine if that was true.

It was scary, sitting in a secret meeting, but Irena believed strongly in what she was doing. Everyone would jump at a sudden noise outside, hold their breath until it passed. But the menacing tread of Nazi boots did motivate cooperation between activists all along the political spectrum. They might be "left" and "right" believers, but they were patriots. They joined to create a covert Polish government and army. They published resistance newspapers to spread subversive news and hope.

But even the brightest hope did not feed hungry people. Irena's professor, Dr. Radlinska, had gone underground in fear for her life, and it was the same with Dr. Hirszfeld, Ala's mentor and medical research partner, and Dr. Witwicki, the Polish psychologist who mentored Irena's friend Ewa Rechtman. The party needed couriers to deliver them money to live on. If discovered by the Germans, both the hidden and the couriers would likely face death.

*"Any volunteers?"*

Eyebrows shot up when Irena volunteered. She was small, less than five foot tall, and she readily admitted her full, rosy cheeks made her look younger than her years. But Irena had backbone. She did not slouch at danger, not when her friends' lives were at risk.

Irena walked with confident purpose down Gesia Street carrying the secret package for delivery. Behind her rang the sounds of Jewish city life, street criers calling out in Yiddish, jockeying for the best corner to hawk their wares. The stone streets echoed with the scrape and rattle of the iron wheels on the handcarts. In the distance came the clanking of a tram and the cry of gulls on the bank of the Vistula River.

She hesitated a moment at the doorway marked number one, taking in the spiced aromas of street food and the cold air of late autumn. Then Irena pulled the handbell to the convent of the Sisters of Ursuline. The nun who opened the door and asked her business wore a grave face under her starched wimple.

*I'm here to see Pani Rudnicki, please, Sister.*

The nun nodded and pulled back the bolt on the heavy door. Irena stepped into the shadows of the foyer, and the sister drew the bolt smoothly behind her. Irena followed the sister through the courtyard and along a hall. How strange to visit someone who didn't exist! Mrs. Rudnicki was a fiction. Or, if she had once lived, she did no longer, and in her death released her identity to a desperate stranger. Rudnicki was the false name under which Helena Radlinska was hiding inside this walled convent. Irena may have guessed Dr. Radlinska worked in the resistance. But she had no way of knowing her friend was a senior

Dr. Helena Radlinska.
*Mateusz Opasinski, CC ASA 3.0*

operative in the underground Polish army. The leaders of the resistance worked in isolation, creating secret resistance cells in a network, where, for everyone's protection, few people knew each other's names.

After a quiet knock, Irena entered the room where her old professor waited. The woman's warm grasp invoked a flood of pleasure. Over sweet, milky tea, a Polish staple, Irena and the professor caught up. Finding any good news required effort. Irena knew that the Jews had been banned from receiving state welfare. Even before the war she'd worked with ". . . families where one herring was shared amongst six children during Sabbath." Dr. Radlinska was encouraging. They shared a passion for the most vulnerable people, and they determined to do everything in their power to fight the cruelty of the Nazis. After all, the war wouldn't last forever. And how much worse could things get?

# 3

*Resistance*

## Warsaw, 1940–1941

A lot worse, Irena discovered shortly. She peddled hard, speeding on her bicycle through the streets toward the Czyste hospital on Dworska Street, determined to find Ala.

Reaching the Jewish hospital, Irena paused only a moment to catch her breath and secure her bicycle. The sprawling compound not far from the Vistula River had been one of the most modern medical facilities anywhere in Europe. Now, the nurses and doctors ran short on supplies, and Ala, *brave Ala*, faced an unending stream of bruised, broken, and dying people, almost all of them innocent victims of Nazi anti-Semitism. Irena waited in the corridor, searching the faces of the medical staff rushing to and fro. Finally, she caught sight of Ala, who barely stopped to squeeze Irena's arm.

## Ala Gołab-Grynberg

As a lead nurse in the hospital's ambulance corps, a large part of Ala's job was triage, sorting the injured and sick, deciding who must be treated first, who could wait, who was hopeless. These tough decisions had to be made to increase the number who would survive. Every case could break her heart if she let it.

Ala's professional training and strength of purpose steadied her as she nursed the bloodied bodies of the elderly. Their only crime: too slowly following orders in German accents that they did not understand. For this, they were hauled feet-first behind horse-drawn cabs along cobblestone streets until skulls shattered. She saw men whose beards had been torn from their faces or slashed off by knife blade, and scrawny street children fighting to survive SS beatings. The hospital staff were doing thirty or forty serious operations a day, all without anesthesia. Calm-faced, Ala worked quickly. But inside she felt the furious desperation of a trapped animal.

Sometimes throwing open the broad sash of a hospital window, she leaned far, far out, sucking in the fresh air. She never thought of jumping. But everyone sometimes thought of falling. At home in the darkness, Ala wrote poems on bits of scrap paper and tried to make sense of the jumbled images.

For everything was jumbled, no matter how much she and her nursing staff struggled to make order. Once gleaming hospital wards were now filled with the stench of wounds, frightened patients, and the dull sheen of despair. Artillery fire had blown out the plate glass windows, so sheets and scraps of wood had been tacked up to cover them. By late October, temperatures in the early morning dropped below freezing. The pieced together walls reflected the patched up, shattered bodies, and at the end of her shift Ala's head ached from clenching her jaw in fury.

The fury almost kept her fear away. Fear for these victims of brutality and for her own family. Her husband, Arek, had left Warsaw with the Polish army in September. She'd heard one vague report that someone had seen him on the Eastern Front late that month in bad condition. Her brother Sam and his wife had escaped to Russian territory. Would Arek somehow find them? Worry about her daughter inflamed her deepest fears. She couldn't bear her child's defenseless face to arise in the same thought as those Nazi monsters.

Irena saw clearly that Ala was making a difference, saving lives. In her own sphere of work, Irena formed a plan to do the same. For years already, she had broken the law, quietly subverting the anti-Jewish policies of the Polish government. It wasn't just the Nazis who treated Jewish people worse than others. Some of the rules in Poland were unfair too. She had been altering names and dates in order to give poor Jewish families benefits.

Now, Irena decided to broaden her scheme. She would need help. With the Germans in charge, this would be a much more serious crime than fraud. She could not ask just anyone. She knew she could trust her boss, Irka, and two friends who also worked in the social welfare offices came to mind. Jadwiga Deneka and Jaga Piotrowska had gone to school at the Polish Free University too.

One evening, Irena invited the three women to the second-floor flat in the Wola district on Ludwiki Street where she lived with her mother. Circled around her small kitchen table, they spoke in low voices. Jadwiga, a vivacious woman with a pixie bob, worked in an innovative orphanage school. Jaga's job was finding homes for orphans. The sturdy, short woman with dark eyes was old-fashioned, and, unlike Irena, a devout Catholic. But they had become allies in their passion for helping the poor, and through Jaga's younger sister, Janka. Where Jaga was straight-laced and sincere, Janka was irreverent and ironic. She and Irena were fast friends, which strengthened Irena's faith in Jaga.

That night the women decided on a small but perilous act of resistance. They agreed they would quietly defy the Nazis anti-Jewish directives. Making simple changes to their paperwork, they would carry on as usual helping all their clients. They had no grand plan or overarching vision, just Irena's stubborn desire to help suffering people.

Their system was simple, yet brilliant. The Polish social services distributed food, money, and clothing based on data collected through interviews with families in poor communities. Irena's job even before the war had been conducting these interviews, which provided the statistics to warrant aid. Now, she and other staff would forge these statistics and interviews. They would compile lists of made-up names, non-Jewish names, to requisition funds that they would stealthily distribute through Irena's soup kitchens.

"So we forged these statistics and interviews—meaning we listed made-up names, and in this way were able to secure money, food items, clothing," which they passed out at the centers.

To discourage the Nazis from checking up on their fictitious families, the young women cheerfully added to the dossiers ominous notations about deadly communicable diseases like typhus and cholera. The small offices hummed with activity and shared glances.

By the fall of 1940, the small team was providing public welfare support to thousands of Jews in Warsaw. Irena had longed for adventure. Now she worked secretly, in plain sight, foiling the Nazis. Though risking torture and death, she felt fiercely alive.

### *Ein Jude!* A Jew!

One decree after another, the German occupiers cinched their grip on Poland's Jews. They established a council, Judenräte, of rabbis and other influential men in the

Jewish community, and they charged this Judenräte with the immediate and precise execution of all Nazi orders, including registration of all Jews by age and profession and a survey of all Jewish-owned property. The Judenräte Council leaders hoped the Germans would lose the war, and assumed temporary cooperation would lead to survival and eventual liberation.

But for now, Jews could not own radios or enter movie theaters. Jews twelve and older must wear white armbands with a blue Star of David on their sleeve whenever they went out in public. This allowed SS officers to immediately identify them. Men were kidnapped and deported for slave labor; women were snagged off the street and forced to do cleaning chores for the SS.

The Germans closed Warsaw's synagogues and enforced a 5:00 p.m. curfew for Jews. Jews could not send letters overseas, use telephones or trains, walk in the city's parks, or sit on municipal benches. Jewish doctors could not treat Polish patients, and Polish doctors were forbidden to treat Jewish patients. The regime seized Jew's bank accounts, allowing them to withdraw only two hundred zlotys a week, and not to possess at any time more than two thousand zlotys in cash. At that time two hundred zlotys was the equivalent of only six hundred dollars today, only enough for the basics.

The occupying soldiers broke into Jewish businesses and looted them, knocked on doors of homes and came in looking for anything worth stealing, carrying away baskets and boxes of valuables or essentials like bedding. If they liked the look of a place, they evicted the family and moved right in.

Perhaps most galling, sometimes a mean-spirited or envious fellow Polish citizen outed Jews whose physical features had not already betrayed them. *"Ein Jude!"* they sang out, pointing their fingers and identifying them to the Nazis. Blackmailers and thugs accosted men or boys they guessed might be Jewish and ordered them to drop their pants. When they found a male who was circumcised, a surgery proscribed by Jewish law and rare among Polish Christians, they freely attacked and even killed him. Anti-Semitic Poles joined the Nazis smashing Jewish shop windows and randomly attacking Jews on the streets, beating them to death for sport and entertainment.

In March 1940, Germans labeled the major Jewish neighborhood "A Plague-Infected Area," and on March 27, the Judenräte was ordered to build a wall around it.

For centuries, Poland had been home to the largest and most significant Jewish community in the world, with Warsaw its center. Despite long-standing persecution and these new restrictions, Jews in Warsaw and their Polish friends believed that there were limits to what could possibly happen. War was hard, of course. Terrible things happened to individuals. But so far, the Germans had arrested and executed Poles in their purges. The first systematic anti-Semitic edicts were primarily financial, and Irena's friends and many other Jewish people in Warsaw had been lulled into a sense of relative security.

On October 3, 1940, Jewish people celebrated the beginning of their new year, Rosh Hashanah, and following, on October 12, came their most holy day, Yom Kippur. All Jews over the age of nine had fasted since before sundown the previous night. They woke early to begin prayer and penitence, for it was the Day of Atonement. To make amends for their sins against God over the past twelve months, Jewish families planned to spend much of the day in prayer. They would fast from work, food, and drink (even water) until nightfall. Already there was tension. The Germans had forbidden all public worship, and a number of Jews had decided they would defy the order and meet in secret.

As many were rising from sleep that morning, loud-speakers squawked outside their windows. Jewish leaders, the Judenräte, heard the news from city officials, but ordinary people heard it blaring in the street. It was the most sweeping edict yet. Every Jew in Warsaw must move into one small section of the city. They had two weeks. There would be no exceptions.

# 4

# Segregated and Isolated

## Lines Drawn—October 1940

Panic gripped the Jewish community at news of the Nazis' latest command. The Nazis' order meant nearly one in four Warsaw families had to pick up household and move to another part of the city. *Let them fight for table scraps among themselves.* That was, more or less, the German position.

On October 16, 1940, posters went up across Warsaw. Anxious residents pulled their coats tighter against the biting wind and huddled around the street signs to read them. Newspapers in Warsaw printed a map showing the new area for Jews, as well as designated Polish and German quarters in Warsaw. The Nazis did not use the term "ghetto," which for hundreds of years had connoted the segregation and restriction of Jews in European cities. They used the term "Jewish Quarter." The official explanation was that the Jewish area would be quarantined to prevent the spread of typhus.

Irena knew that poverty, not ethnicity, spread disease. With her Jewish friends and clients, she eyed the map with suspicion but also with grim determination. People would need to find homes within the allotted space, in the minds of many already a ghetto. Zlota Street, where her office was located, straddled the southern edge of the Jewish area, and her apartment in Wola was just to the east of the district. *What if her apartment had been on the wrong side of the boundary?* She knew it was just chance. The thought of moving her frail mother terrified her. She worried constantly about her mother's health.

The boundaries followed the city's traditional Jewish neighborhood in the heart of Warsaw: starting two blocks west of Marszalkowska Street and two blocks north of Jerusalem Avenue, the city's two most important streets. But 30 percent of Warsaw's current population, some 400,000 people, would be crammed into less than 3 percent of its area. Jewish refugees streaming in from other parts of Poland would also need to find a place to live within the confines.

Irena told her clients that the Judenräte had offered to set up a clearinghouse to match families, but the effort was useless. There simply was not enough housing in the ghetto. On both sides of the new boundary, greedy landlords preyed upon the most desperate would-be tenants, and families often spent days frantically searching for any accommodation, no matter how cramped or dilapidated.

Throughout the last two weeks of October, the moment Irena ventured from her office building she fell in with the jostling crowd, Jewish and Gentile families both—Jews ordered in and Poles ordered out. Throngs of people moved their belongings in handcarts, even baby carriages. Soldiers with guns and rough voices kept the snaking lines in order. Young mothers struggled to carry unwieldy bundles of rolled up linens and bedding, and even small children dragged along towering suitcases. Distraught families realized they must quickly sell what they owned or leave many of their largest and most treasured possessions behind.

Irena's Jewish friends joined the frantic scramble. Ewa Rechtman; Ala and her small daughter, Rami; Rachela Rosenthal and her little girl; Dr. Hirszfeld; Jozef, Theodora, and little Piotr Zysman. They would all have to make sure they had an apartment on the "right" side of the Nazi boundaries. As people feverishly looked for apartments, quarrels erupted about the exact dividing lines of the Jewish Quarter. Poles haggled for their businesses and industrial plants to be exempt. Christians did not want to give up this street or that street because of a church or business. People tried to trade apartments, but in truth there was a shortage everywhere due to buildings destroyed by bombs and the Germans moving in. Piece by piece, street by street, the boundaries shrank.

Irena had seen work started some time ago on a ten-foot-high brick wall down the middle of Zlota Street. The Jewish community was forced to pay for the construction, and Jewish men and boys were forced into labor crews and set to slapping mortar and laying bricks.

Despite the difficulties of the move, many in the Jewish community decided they would be safer in the ghetto, away from the Nazis and their often anti-Semitic Polish neighbors. Besides, friends assured each other, *We'll still meet at each other's apartments, just as always. We'll still live, after all, in the same city.* Irena hoped it was true of her and her friends.

Some parts of the ghetto were grander, like Sienna Street, which was lined with gracious, well-kept buildings. The wealthiest members of the Jewish community snapped up those apartments. Irena's friends were among the privileged few, affluent and assimilated into Polish culture. While Ala and her husband, Arek, were proud Zionists, committed to the establishment of a Jewish state in Palestine, others had not actively practiced Judaism for decades. Her friends Adam and Jozef thought of themselves as Polish more than Jewish. But all of Irena's friends had graduate degrees and professional careers. They all spoke Polish fluently, and perhaps most fortunately, they had a wide network of contacts outside Jewish circles.

Irena's friends moved to the better parts of the area and tried to be optimistic. Money could buy considerable protection from want and deprivation. Other parts of the new quarter offered grim pickings. Haphazard boundaries with crazy corners enclosed blocks crumbled by German aerial bombings.

Traditional and Orthodox Jews, those who kept the old practices and language, had often already lived in poverty. Some were Irena's secret clients. Others had come to Warsaw as refugees, empty handed. Few spoke Polish or had made friends with Catholic neighbors. Now they moved in to any livable space they found. Three, four, even five families might cramp into one small, scruffy apartment. Their large families shared toilets down the hall and fought for floor space to sleep. Disease spread easily in crowded conditions, and the young and the old were especially vulnerable.

A scattering of Jews simply refused to move to the ghetto. A friend of Irena, and part of her secret welfare-fraud network, Maria Palester, had been born Catholic. Her husband, Dr. Henryk Palester, was a Jewish convert, but Maria argued for a bold course of action. The Germans had until now overlooked his conversion because Henryk had a Catholic birth certificate and baptism records. That gave the couple and their two children—a middle-school-aged daughter, Malgorzata, and a teenaged son, Krystof—a rare opportunity. If they could find a way to make a living, they might escape detection. Like all registered Jews in Warsaw, Henryk had been fired from his state job. He'd been a physician working as a specialist in infectious diseases for the Polish government's health ministry.

Irena wanted to help and managed to arrange a job for Maria in the welfare offices. Maria would support the family, and the Palesters would carry on—in their own apartment, under their own names—as if they were just any other Polish family. They did not disavow Henryk's Judaism. They just didn't tell the Germans about it.

Maria also persuaded her Jewish neighbor and friend Maria Proner—a professor and the mother of a preteen daughter—to risk living on the Aryan side. Maria was already certain that the ghetto was a trap set for the Jewish community. Something in her gut told her there was terrible danger. She was not going to spend the war skulking around and hiding out in her apartment, either. On the contrary, it was a game of confidence, she figured. The best bet was to hide in the open. Fear was a gambler's tell, and Maria was a spunky and experienced card player. When her regular bridge game turned out to include some Gestapo informers and even some ethnic German *Volksdeutsche*, she made a point of being charming and vivacious. It wouldn't hurt to have connections if they were discovered, and everyone knew bribes could solve all sorts of problems.

## Ghetto Closed—November 1940

A new order was announced from the governor of the Warsaw district, Dr. Ludwig Fischer, on November 10. It read in part,

Recently Jews who left their designated district have spread cases of spotted fever. In order to forestall danger to population it is decreed that a Jew who leaves his designated district without authorization will be subject to the death penalty.

The same penalty will apply to anyone who consciously gives help to such a Jew (for example, by making available a night's lodging, food, offering transportation of any kind, etc.) . . . it will be applied with merciless severity.

The next Saturday morning, Jewish families prepared for underground religious services. Mothers nagged their children to button up in their coats. "Wear your scarf," they said. "Don't forget your hat." They braved the ghetto, walking slowly, ducking into cellars, or climbing steep stairs to rooms under the eaves. No doubt, parents told their children stories of Jews celebrating *Shabbat* in other bitter times and places.

The crowded streets filled with shouts and a growing noisy commotion. Children stood on tiptoe trying to see what had happened. The news flew through the crowd

A Jewish policeman speaks with a woman on the street in the Warsaw ghetto, 1941. *United States Holocaust Memorial Museum, courtesy of Günther Schwarberg*

faster than the dreaded typhus. Alarm pulsed through the crowds as people in the Jewish district realized they were penned in on all sides. Accused of spreading disease, the Jews in the ghetto were walled off from the world like animals unfit for human society.

Soldiers stood guard at the gates. No one was allowed in or out. Officially, there were twenty-two openings in the ghetto walls. Now, each had a sentry post manned by one German officer, one Polish "Blue" policeman, and one man from the Jewish ghetto police. Many in the quarter scoffed at these traitors, while some thought having their own officers provided at least a bit of safety.

Some wily and brave ghetto residents talked their way through the checkpoints that first day or found breaks in the wall. The barrier blocked streets, cut through the middle of buildings or along back alleys. It blocked off windows, doors, and gaps between buildings.

The guarded gates came as a thunderbolt, a sudden approaching darkness, a rumble of foreboding. But the resourceful broke out to bring back food in the coming days. And as word spread across Warsaw, Polish residents—both friends and strangers—crowded at the walls with supplies of bread and gifts of flowers. These they handed through the gates or tossed over the barbed wire that ran along the top of the three-meter brick barricade.

In the early days of the ghetto, the homemaker's daily ritual might have included a walk outside the boundaries to city markets to buy food for their families. The women made sure to remember their ration cards. Often they fretted. How much food would the precious few cards allow them today? Which stalls in the market had the best deals?

Now they depended on the few shipments of fresh produce allowed in from the "Aryan" side and hastily organized ghetto markets. Whole families searched for food at the makeshift market stalls that sprang up out of canvas-covered wagons or on rickety tables. When goods in the market ran out, smugglers sold food and other necessities at outrageous prices. For hungry families, shopping day was a nightmare.

In wartime, everything was hard to get, and so the new rulers doled out food according to daily rations. But how much food people got from rations depended on what "race" was listed on your *kennkarte*. Jewish people got the least of all. Their official rations did not cover even 10 percent of the requirements for a normal diet. Irena was aghast when she learned that the official rations allotted her Jewish friends was a paltry 184 daily calories. People would starve without the underground economy that sprang up with smugglers dealing in basic foodstuffs and selling any product that someone would buy.

Cunning, the smugglers found that small and nimble children could slip out through gaps or climb the perimeter of the wall. Those under age twelve did not have to wear an armband and were not so visible on the Aryan

Street children in the Warsaw ghetto, 1941. *United States Holocaust Memorial Museum, courtesy of Günther Schwarberg*

Ghetto market, 1940–1943. *Yad Vashem*

side. Germans responded by ordering the Jews to build the wall higher—and to pay for the costs of the construction. They added loops of barbed wire and broken bottle tops to the walls, and made sport of shooting children caught sneaking in food.

Prices rocketed, filling the streets with beggars and starving the poorest. Men wept in the streets pleading for bread. Within weeks, cold, disease, and hunger turned the place into a cemetery for the living. The German governor of Warsaw boasted that starvation was simply official policy: "The Jews will die from hunger and destitution and a cemetery will remain of the Jewish question."

Once the Jewish population of Warsaw was rounded up and imprisoned, Jewish refugees from other areas arrived. Across German-occupied Poland, the Nazis had dissolved Jewish villages and towns. Those people who survived were relocated to cities, and now they were deported to the Warsaw ghetto. More than a half million people crowded within its guarded walls.

# 5

## Life in the Ghetto

### Smugglers—1940–1941

Irena steadied her nerves and lifted her chin as she walked up to the gate on Leszno Street near the Great Synagogue. SS squads with guns resting on their hips scrutinized her papers. They peppered her with questions and as always, seemed to relish barking orders. Today, she carried her most valuable secret cargo—typhus vaccination—each tiny illicit vial capable of saving a life.

Sometimes Irena stitched money into her clothes, or padded her brassiere with contraband, having sewn small pockets inside the undergarment. Many women had done the same, joking about how, since the Nazi occupation of Warsaw, women's breasts appeared to have grown bigger. Or more whimsically, she sneaked in wooden dolls, sculpted by one of her former professors, Dr. Witwicki. He spent his days in hiding making toys for the littlest ones at Dr. Korczak's orphanage in the ghetto.

Irena joined the ranks of ghetto smugglers, not for profit but to help her imprisoned friends and the poor families she had secretly aided before they had moved into the ghetto. "The first time I went into the ghetto it made a hellish impression on me," said Irena. "I'd go out in the morning on my rounds and see a starving child lying there. I'd come back a few hours later and he'd be dead . . . covered with a newspaper."

Due to the hardship she saw in the ghetto, Irena felt it little enough to risk her life at the checkpoint. Though her sanitation job was a fiction, when the sentries demanded her papers, she was able to present a legitimate pass. She came each day as many times as she could, carried along by the tide of people, striving to be as forgettable as the laundry flapping from upstairs windows in the autumn wind. She chose to enter and exit from different guard posts in careful rotation, so as not to arouse suspicion. Anyone caught helping Jews, even giving them a bite to eat, invited arrest and likely deportation to a work camp, which might be more accurately called a "work-to-death" camp.

Dr. Juliusz Majkowski, a friend working for the city to keep ahead of communicable disease in Warsaw, authorized Irena to enter the ghetto. He added her, Irka Schultz, and Jadwiga Deneka to his list of medical corps workers and issued them epidemic control passes. The Nazis, terrified of infectious disease, left the job of virus control to "dispensable" Polish people.

Once through the gate, Irena pulled her overcoat tight against the cold and pinned on her sleeve a blue Star of David. It some other cities, the stars were yellow, but it was always a blue star in Warsaw. It was a small gesture to show solidarity with Ala, Ewa, and her other Jewish friends. Cutting through the people, a constant throng on the ghetto streets, Irena blocked from her mind images of how this street used to look before the war, when it was a happy bustle of middle-class houses and Jewish shops. Today residents scuttled along the edges of the buildings, pressing themselves as far away as possible from the guards and their unpredictable tempers. Further along, the Germans had turned the street's grand synagogue into a barn to store fodder and a rank horse stable.

Irena hastened to Sienna Street, one of the richest and most lively parts of the Jewish Quarter. Making her way through the crowd to number 16, she opened the door to the youth center and Ewa's office. Arriving breathless, her cheeks red from the bitter wind, Irena called out a greeting. She had undone her scarf and buttons by the time Ewa crossed the room. Grinning, Irena opened her palm to show her the precious medicine.

Ewa Rechtman had once been a language student, one of the most talented scholars in the linguistics program at the Polish Free University. Now a prisoner in the ghetto, she worked with CENTOS, a Jewish self-help charity, getting hold of food for the poor, which was usually no more than once-a-day soup and black bread.

Ewa clapped her hands with pleasure and seized Irena in a generous hug. In her quiet, lilting voice, Ewa called the dozen or so teenagers and children in the room to gather for an announcement. Irena thought everything Ewa said sounded like a lullaby. She had no hard edges, even in these terrible times. Ewa had always been clever and capable, and she appeared unfaltering in her work here with the children. CENTOS provided child care, and Irena suspected Ewa was often up all night nursing toddlers sick with typhus or cholera. A lump rose in Irena's throat seeing Ewa so thin; her tumble of dark curls tied back revealed the overly prominent bones of her face and neck.

With a solemn expression in her dark eyes, Ewa held up the three vials for the boys and girls to see. "Who should get the vaccinations?" she asked.

*And how should the choice be made?*

Ewa left them on their own to make this life and death decision. The youngsters huddled, deliberating, and reaching a quick and unanimous agreement. Two orphan boys in charge of younger siblings, and the girl in the youth circle who worked the hardest would be vaccinated.

Irena also stopped by to see Rachela and her youth circle, one of the largest and liveliest in the ghetto, on Pawiak Street, a traditionally Jewish area even before the ghetto lines were drawn. Rachela lived in one of the large apartment buildings there with her daughter, who was close in age to Ala's little Rami. She organized playgroups and makeshift entertainment for the small children on Pawiak Street, which had become one of the grimmest in the ghetto. More than twenty-five thousand people crammed into buildings there. Plumbing could not handle the human waste of the crowded buildings, and often it was thrown back into the yards or street to accumulate with growing heaps of rubbish and vermin. And on one of the street's corners stood the Gestapo-run prison, a true house of horrors, called Pawiak after the street. Rachela's youth circle, her charm, affectionate nature, and sense of fun, her bedrock belief in the power of children's laughter created an oasis for the innocent in the harsh, bleak neighborhood.

Ogrodowa Street was another stop on Irena's smuggled goods delivery route. Jozef, Irena's lawyer friend from the courthouse hallways, it seemed a lifetime ago, supervised the youth activities there in "midtown" ghetto, near the Jewish police headquarters. Many former lawyers and judges saw a chance to make money and curry favor with the Nazis, so they pinned on the police badge with zeal. These officers disgusted Jozef; they patrolled the ghetto walls like thugs, bribing and blackmailing their fellow Jews. Even worse, the officers helped the Gestapo kidnap people for slave labor.

Jozef, along with Irena's close friend Adam and Ala's

husband, Arek, also joined the Jewish resistance movement. Jozef and a small group of trusted friends ran an underground press, printing and secretly distributing newspapers and pamphlets urging citizens to resist the invaders, whether inside or outside the compound. This cell met to make plans in a garden toolshed on Leszno Street, out behind the old rectory at St. Mary's.

The Catholic church grounds straddled the ghetto wall, and secret passageways led from one side to the other. At the end of the long garden, sitting on overturned clay pots long after curfew, the conspirators plotted how best to get their illegal publications out to the people without getting caught by the Germans. Hope burned a little stronger on those nights when a small, fearless Polish woman, code name Jolanta, crept through the shadows to join them, and shared her determination to defy the Nazis at any cost. Only her friends knew that the woman called Jolanta was really Irena.

## Ala Gołab-Grynberg

In the darkness of early morning, Ala kissed her small, sleeping daughter Rami good-bye, her heart aching with the knowledge that she might not return alive. Leaving her parents Moshe and Rachel, and her older brother, Janek, she hurried out into the cold.

Winter had arrived early in 1941, bringing snow in October. It caught children in the ghetto with no shoes, no coats, their clothes in rags. That first night some seventy froze to death. Each morning, the dead lined the streets, piled naked and covered with old newsprint and stones. The threads they had worn were taken by the living, who desperately needed warmth. Rats gnawed at the corpses.

Bodies also lined the streets like garbage each morning after SS men used pedestrians for target practice. Shots rang out at all hours, echoing off the buildings, followed by heartrending cries and wailing, or long, empty quiet. Later in the day, coming home, Ala would need to push through crowded streets, bumping elbows with skeletal children, anguishing over their sunken eyes and hollow cheeks, their thin fingers reaching, croaking voices begging.

"Bread. Just a piece of bread."

Some had no strength to beg in the noisy streets. They sat covered with flies and fleas, collapsed and crying by the corpses of their parents. Ala shuddered. Crazy how you could get used to such sights, used to stepping over the dead bodies of children.

She didn't have to read the underground newspapers to know, "Abuses—wild, bestial 'amusements'—are daily events," in the Jewish sector. The soldiers remained untouched by the affliction, entertaining themselves with killing, beating, and humiliating their victims. Dr. Hirszfeld said, "Most nations would weep to see such misery, but the German soldiers laugh."

Working with Dr. Hirszfeld at the Jewish hospital as

the chief of nursing, Ala hated having to help patch up after the soldiers' sadism. The doctor said he saw, "A child smuggler caught by a German and begging, 'Don't kill me.' The German soldier told him, 'Don't worry, I will only make sure you won't smuggle again'. . . and he shot the child in both legs. Later they had to be amputated."

Thousands of children depended on smuggling to eat. They made their way in and out holes in the ghetto wall, which they camouflaged with loose bricks. Or emaciated children slipped through wire or past a loosened plank in places where only a wooden fence or barbed wire stood between them and the Aryan side. Though, of course, the merciless soldiers were ever-present.

Dr. Hirszfeld told of how Germans loved dogs and would stop to pet one while walking away from Jews they had just shot dead. A Jewish child said, "I would like to be a dog and I wouldn't be afraid that they would kill me."

Hurrying through the snowy streets toward the Twarda Gate, Ala checked to make sure she had her papers, her pass in and out of the ghetto. In the beginning, just after the ghetto exits were closed, the Jewish hospital ended up on the Aryan side of the border. That meant every morning nurses like Ala and doctors like Dr. Hirszfeld had to go through a checkpoint. The doctor hunched in his overcoat against the bitter morning cold, his tufts of white hair peeking out from beneath a dignified fedora. Ala whispered a greeting and huddled

Irena's friend and collaborator, Ala Gołab-Grynberg, chief nurse of the Warsaw ghetto.
*Courtesy of the Gołab-Grynberg Family*

Dr. Ludwik Hirszfeld.
*Yad Vashem*

with her hospital coworkers waiting at the checkpoint.

At precisely 7 a.m., Ala and the hospital staff stepped up to the corner of Twarda and Zlota streets, where they would exit under guard. Passing soldiers pushed their bicycles along the cobblestones. It was just the start of another workday for them, too, fitted out in their helmets and brass-buttoned overcoats, their guns casually flung across their chests.

Plastered at the gate was a sign that all the doctors and nurses found loathsome. In German and Polish it warned: TYPHUS INFECTION AREA, AUTHORIZED PASSAGE ONLY. Beside her, Dr. Hirszfeld growled. He often railed at this Nazi propaganda. The lying rats had created ideal conditions in the ghetto for a typhus epidemic. It was because of the ghetto that this disease was happening.

Waiting her turn at the gate, Ala craned her neck. Irena's welfare office was a few blocks up Zlota Street, though she wouldn't catch a glimpse of her friend. A review of the office files had raised Nazis suspicions, and they had already transferred Irena to a satellite facility distant from the ghetto.

Finally, Ala presented her documents for inspection, and the group passed through the gate under guard. The short, quick march to the hospital was terrifying. Spying a handful of young SS men sauntering toward the medical group, the doctors and nurses dropped their eyes to the ground quickly and tried not to shrink in fear, but it made no difference.

*Whack.* A rifle butt hit the chest of a doctor at the front of the team. He fell, and then came the sound of boots thudding on bone and the doctor's cries. Then, more rifle butts. More boots, more agonized moans. A flurry of gray green uniforms. German words, laughter. Passersby scurrying away. The SS shouting at the doctors. *Get off the ground, line up, jumping jacks, faster, faster* . . . until the tormented doctors toppled over. Howling with glee, the SS men moved on, seeking fresh entertainment.

It had happened before. It would happen again. As she made the march, Ala zeroed her mind on her patients. The terrified, bruised, and broken picked themselves up and continued their way to the hospital.

Irena was aghast at the willy-nilly attacks on anyone Jewish. Of all her friends in the ghetto, Ala was the most fearless and brazen. But could even Ala's courage withstand such brutal treatment? Her and Irena's friendship had deepened as times grew more troubled. One more Nazi sanction closed the Jewish hospital that December, but Irena felt relieved her friend would no long walk this gauntlet.

The medical teams, including Ala, now staffed smaller clinics scattered throughout the ghetto. Ghetto residents could see a doctor or nurse without getting a border pass, but the clinics could not possibly meet the overwhelming need. Today she had come with Ala to one of the secret classes her friend helped organized in the hope that information could help slow the spread of disease.

Irena shivered with cold and refocused her attention. *Rickettsia prowazekii. Bacterium. Pediculus humanus humanus.* Louse infection. The room was crowded with young men and women scratching cramped notes in the dark on precious paper. Dr. Landau emphasized to the group that cleanliness could combat the typhus epidemic raging through the Jewish community. Irena glanced across the room and exchanged a worried look with Ala. Even some of their friends had taken sick.

Dr. Landau drummed his chalk against the makeshift blackboard. Yes, it was challenging with the cramped quarters, the lack of adequate sewage disposal, and people's poor health in general—but too many people were dying.

One candle labored to light the room. In the shadows, Dr. Landau taught this forbidden gathering of teenagers every bit of information he knew that might help stop the barrage of disease. His firm, gruff manner reminded Irena of a sergeant or maybe a general. And in fact, besides these health lectures, the doctor led paramilitary medical training for the young men and women in the ghetto beginning to plan for armed resistance against the Germans.

*Two. Thousand. People*—the doctor punched each word—*have died this month. We must work*—

Heavy boots stomped close outside breaking even the doctor's concentration for a moment. A pencil dropped, rolled across the floor, too loud in the sudden silence.

Outside the window Nazi voices bellowed orders. *Raus! Juden Raus! Heraustreten! Out! Jews out! Come out!*

A child's scream pierced the hostile air. Window glass reverberated amidst gunshots.

Everyone turned to Dr. Landau. Where could they hide? Dr. Landau's staunch gaze pinned them in place, his voice never faltered as he went on. Infection occurs when the feces of the *Rickettsia prowazekii bacterium* . . .

The Nazis' tread faded and a girl burst into sobs, gasping for breath in spasms of hysteria. Others, shaken, started crying, too. Dr. Landau turned on them. "Don't you people understand yet?" Students' eyes widened at his fierce tone. Only Ala looked calm. Irena swelled with pride in her friend.

"All of us, every day and every night are on the front lines," the doctor said. "We are the battle troops in a war that never stops. We are soldiers. We must be tough. There is no crying allowed here!"

With a tap of the chalk, he turned back to the blackboard and picked up his chain of thought. A burst of white dust hung for a moment in the air. No one dared cough, lest the doctor think they were sniffling. The only sound came from pencils scribbling notes in the dusky room and the doctor's calm voice continuing the lesson.

Irena watched Ala nodding at the doctor's words. Her friend's black eyes remained sharp as ever, but she was rail thin. Her ill-fitting clothes hung from her shoulders. Irena knew the widespread suffering crushed Ala, who worried about family. Her husband, Arek, lucky to survive the Eastern Front, made his way home only to flee to the forest outside Warsaw and join the resistance fighters. Organizing these secret classrooms was a small part of Ala, an effort to help alleviate the suffering. She also led a youth circle at number 9 Smocza Street, in between her duty hours at one or other of the medical clinics.

At refugee centers and in the hospitals, staff fought disease and starvation every day. But Irena sensed not everyone in the ghetto was struggling, especially not in the wealthy districts. Ala and Ewa told her that was true.

"Ghetto aristocrats"—rich industrialists, many Judenräte leaders, Jewish police officers, profiteering smugglers, nightclub owners—danced among the corpses, partying at more than sixty cafés and nightclubs in the ghetto. The Sienna Street complex where Ewa worked housed one of those cafés, where the bands played on, accompanied to raucous singing. Because the café was only a stone's throw from the relocated Czyste hospital's main ward, now at number 1 Leszno Street, many of the doctors and nurses went there after hours.

Ala came from a well-known family of actors and directors and occasionally visited the nightclubs. She had a famous relative who performed at Café Sztuka, her cousin-by-marriage, Weronika Grynberg, better known in Warsaw as the sultry cabaret actress with the stage name Vera Gran. *Come with me*, a grinning Ala sometimes urged

Irena. *Spend the night in the ghetto and see what goes on at Café Sztuka.*

Irena risked her life several times a day already. It felt energizing and electric. Risking it again to spend the evening with friends hardly seemed to make a difference. The danger seemed remote and abstract, and so one night she walked into Café Sztuka with her friends and sat down for a drink. It was forbidden, of course, and she would have been shot had she been discovered, but for a moment Irena could enjoy her friends and make believe life would go on as it had before the war.

In the smoky darkness of the café that evening, Vera Gran crooned away. A prewar starlet, Vera's voice quickly became a popular attraction at Café Sztuka, number 2 Leszno Street, a few yards inside the ghetto gates. Her duets with pianist Wladyslaw Szpilman drew huge, appreciative crowds, including nightly visits from Ala's mentor, Dr. Hirszfeld, a devoted Café Sztuka regular.

But Irena's imagination could only stretch so far. She couldn't ignore the Gestapo officers, Judenräte elite, and SS men casually blowing rings of smoke, their eyes dreamy and wistful as Vera belted out sad love songs. Waiters sloshed champagne into their waiting glasses, and giddy women in elegant prewar finery stumbled past small tables. Someone placed a plate of salmon hors d'oeuvres in front of Irena. She could not bring herself to eat it amid the brittle tinkle of drunken laughter.

Irena knew that compassion lay behind some entertainment put on for the ghetto rich, and raised money for the needy. Teenagers at Ala's youth center performed plays for the wealthy residents and donated the ticket revenues to buy black-market food and medicines for children. When Dr. Korczak's orphanage needed a fund-raiser, Ala persuaded her husband's celebrity cousin to sing at a benefit, and as always Vera Gran drew huge audiences with her alluring talent. Classical musicians organized an orchestra. "In a darkened room we sat motionless, deeply moved. I never missed a symphony," said one ghetto dweller, "but then the Germans closed it."

Part of Vera Gran's attraction was the power of her voice, but it didn't hurt that Vera was also beautiful. Underneath that silky exterior, though, was a hard-bitten and vicious woman, one of the ghetto's most determined survivors. She didn't sing only in the ghetto. Vera was also the star attraction at Café Mocha on Marszalkowska Street, in the Aryan quarter, where she entertained enthusiastic Germans, advancing her friendship with the Gestapo.

That night at Café Sztuka, Irena could only look on at this nightmare world. *Everyone is crying*, she thought to herself. Everyone. But they were crying for all the wrong reasons. When she left the steamy, warm café, racks of fur coats lined the foyer. Outside the door, half-frozen children lay dying.

# 6

## Raising the Stakes

**1941–1942**

Irena had always craved the hum of activity, but now she needed it to stay positive. This war had turned the world upside down. Just months ago, she could not have imagined the brutality of the German troops, the depravity of the Nazi regime. She needed to be taking some kind of action to have any hope.

The work Irena, Jaga, Jadwiga, and Irka did in secret—forging welfare benefits—was becoming more and more dangerous. The Gestapo had scoured the welfare offices, and one supervisor had been deported to a concentration camp in the east called Auschwitz. The friends' urgent discussion now often focused on safety measures. All of them, including Jaga's sister Janka, continued their smuggling trips to the ghetto. They all used code names for safety. Jadwiga Deneka chose the name Kasia. Irena was Jolanta.

Now, Irena had another, even more daring, idea brewing.

The terrible bombing of Warsaw left thousands of starving orphans homeless on the streets. Hundreds of Jewish children escaped to the Aryan side, trying to survive by begging and stealing, but desperate families had started sending well-loved but starving children across the wall. The winter grew colder than any in recent memory.

Irena and her friends had done well enough faking the documents to funnel food and money to starving Jewish families. Could they fake documents to create *Polish* identities for children who escaped from the ghetto?

The stakes would be high.

They would need to bring more people into the network. The risk of getting caught grew with every person they drew into the circle, and they now had more than a dozen collaborators. Once again they would have to decide whom they could trust. They would have to decide about one man, named Jan Dobraczyński, a Polish Catholic senior official in the Warsaw welfare program.

Jan had overseen placement of Polish orphans and Polish street children in local institutions. When the Nazis had come in and purged the office administration, they promoted Jan to director of the Adult and Child Protective Care Unit. Now he oversaw more than a dozen institutions and several thousand welfare recipients. "For an absurdly low salary I had to be stuck in the office ten hours," he said, though he quickly found a way around it. "Of course I was

Children gathered on a street corner in the Warsaw ghetto, 1942.
*United States Holocaust Memorial Museum, courtesy of Simon Adelman*

not sitting there for ten hours: I tried to be in the office at the beginning and at the end of work day." What he did in between, the Nazis never seemed to notice. His office completed intake interviews and reviewed birth certificates and baptismal records. Children with the correct paperwork came and went in a tidy fashion, sent onward to safe places across the city. Jewish children and their records had no business in Jan's office. But Jewish children had become Irena's primary focus.

Despite Jan's loyalty to Poland, Irena didn't trust him. For years, he had been an active member of an ultra-nationalist and right-wing political party, the same party behind riots at the University of Warsaw when she'd been a student there. Those days were sharp in her memory. Who would forget the sight of brass knuckles flying into one's face and the warmth of gushing blood? Seeing people knocked out cold?

The trouble started when Jewish and Catholic students had been segregated in lecture halls. Catholics sat on the right and Jewish students had been forced to the left. Some students staged angry and impassioned demonstrations on campus, and many Jews refused to sit at all during lectures. Some professors wore the green ribbons indicating their support for the racist policy and ordered rebellious students out of the classroom. A few lectured on their feet to show solidarity.

This segregated seating in the classroom was called the bench ghetto, and it incensed Irena, who was quick to stand by her Jewish friends. She remembered the day in autumn of 1935, the laden stillness in the room when the lecture ended, how breathless she'd been as the seconds stretched on. She was twenty-five years old, her full height not reaching five feet. The crowd towered over her.

A sudden movement from the right brought a rush of air as body-met-body. Irena saw a flash of green ribbon, a raised cane, a glimmer of light reflected—*Razor blades!* Irena gasped. *They'd attached razor blades to the canes they were wielding.* Screams erupted as the attackers surged forward, followed by the sound of brass knuckles hitting bone.

One of the thugs shouted at the Jewish classmate next to Irena, a young man with curly dark hair and glasses. "Why are you standing?"

The young man managed a steady voice, even with the cane raised over his head. "Because I am Jewish."

Without warning, a fist blocked Irena's vision. "Why are you standing?"

She jerked to meet his blazing stare with her own. She wanted to madden the hooligan in front of her. "Because," she snapped, "I am Polish."

The brass-covered fist smashed into her face.

Yes, her nose had hurt for a good long time, but Irena did not regret defying the bullies. Later, when she saw

63

the word "Aryan" stamped on her university ID card, she scratched it out in protest. Campus administrators did not tolerate dissent. They slapped Irena with an indefinite university suspension. Not allowed to return, it was several years before she finagled a degree with the help of a sympathetic professor.

Irena felt justified in her suspicion of Jan Dobraczyński. He'd affiliated with those ruffians! Jan believed Poland was for Poles—and in his mind Poles were Catholic. She knew Jan liked to think he was fair minded. But he didn't mind saying there should be some restrictions on *those people*. The Jews controlled entire sections of the economy, shutting out Poles. Of course conflict would arise. What had the Jews expected?

Gathered at Irena's home, in the inner circle of old friends, they could be frank, even when they disagreed. And disagree they did, on the question of Jan Dobraczyński. Jaga's work brought her into regular contact with Jan. She argued they had to think of the possibilities, the many impoverished children who might get a chance at life with documents Jan could provide. For weeks, Irena debated about Jan. She didn't trust him, but she trusted Jaga, and her friend's passionate endorsement meant something. She certainly didn't want to quarrel.

But she could not afford to risk the lives of those in her network. One weak link, one word spoken in a German ear—well, that would be the end. Handbills posted across

Warsaw in the last weeks had made the penalty for helping Jews entirely clear—summary execution.

## Orphan Roundup—January 1942

During wartime, deprivation made no distinction between religion or place of residence. Orphans scrounged food on the streets across Warsaw, inside the ghetto and out. The number of homeless youngsters picked up off the street had doubled in the two years of German occupation. Jan's close friend Jaga Piotrowska worked finding homes for them. In peacetime, Father Boduen, a charity home for Polish infants, toddlers, and homeless mothers, took in six hundred children a year. In 1941 that number doubled. Those twelve hundred waifs were the lucky ones.

What about the orphans still on the street? The German chief of police wanted them rounded up. He called Jan with an ultimatum. These lice-covered beggars were likely carriers of typhus, and the disease was spreading despite Nazi efforts to contain it to the ghetto. Typhus had killed some Germans.

*Delouse the children, and get them off my streets once and for all*, he ordered Jan. Otherwise, the Germans would handle it. Jan didn't like to think about how the Nazis handled things.

Jan passed the job along to the social service field offices, and Jaga sent word to Irena and the others. Together their team swept the city and rounded up the ragamuffins by

Irena Sendler, as a young woman.
*Yad Vashem*

the truckload. They would clean them up, get a doctor to check them over, and then—with Jan's stamp of approval—find some orphanage to take them in.

That winter afternoon, they moved among the boys and girls arriving in streams all day, dozens of skinny little bodies collected at the Nazi's command. In wartime, children didn't giggle or scream with laughter, especially not these children. Homeless urchins lived and died wild on the streets. Any softness and they did not survive.

Irena spoke to the children in a quiet voice, calm and reassuring, but she kept everything moving at a brisk pace when she was in charge of an operation. One by one, the girls in the office cut the children's hair, collected their clothes, and sent them off for a good washing with lye. The harsh soap stung, the youngsters shivered in the unheated room and eyed the adults with suspicion, but they remained eerily quiet.

Jaga and Irena knew that some of these shivering naked boys would be betrayed by their own bodies. Circumcision, the unmistakable proof of Jewish blood, marked one for death. Desperate ghetto children risked their lives to cross the wall, hoping to beg or smuggle enough to feed themselves and often their families. But Irena had not imagined nearly half of the dozens of children would be Jewish.

She'd only just seen Jaga's stricken face when the

German police walked through the door. They wanted to *supervise* a round of baths and delousing. Irena turned frantic eyes to Jaga. Jaga signaled her with a glance toward the back door, then smoothed her dress before going to greet the Nazis. Irena nodded and helped two Jewish boys disappear through the service entrance. Jaga ran interference with soft smiles and agreeable words, then told Irena, *Take them to my parents' house.* Irena raised an eyebrow. *Are you certain?* Jaga shrugged. *What else can we do?*

That night, two frightened orphans slept in a house on Lekarska Street where Jaga lived with her parents, Marian and Celina, her sister Wanda, her husband, Janusz, and their small daughter, Hana. It was a brazen gamble. Jaga's house shared the street with the German war hospital and sentries swarmed night and day.

But the women couldn't take all the children home. When the last truck unloaded that afternoon, they counted thirty-two boys and girls with obvious Jewish looks in one way or another. When facing seemingly impossible dilemmas, Irena couldn't help thinking about her papa. She measured herself against his standards.

When Irena was six years old, an epidemic of typhoid fever broke out in their town, Otwock. The disease thrived in homes without clean drinking water and strong soap for washing. The same homes where parents couldn't afford a doctor for their children. Papa had carried on treating sick and infected patients, telling her, you can't choose not to lend a hand just because it was risky. "You have to stand up to what is wrong in the world," he insisted. "If someone else is drowning, you have to give a hand." Irena knew she couldn't turn these helpless children over to the Germans. Even if Jan might betray them.

Jaga seemed so certain of Jan's goodness. Still Irena hesitated. Hers was not the only life on the line. The Nazis didn't just kill you for aiding Jews. The killed your family, too. How could she risk her mother's life? Her mother knew nothing of her illegal activities.

In the end, she could think of no alternative. Thirty-two youngsters could not disappear through a back entrance in an occupied city. Finding dozens of forged *kennkarte*, the German-issued identity cards, at a moment's notice was impossible. To hide these children in safe places they needed Jan's help. They needed his silence. And Irena would have to trust him.

They would have to go tell Jan what they had discovered. Irena agreed that Jaga would do the talking, for Jaga and Jan had fallen in love, people in the office whispered. He wanted nothing more than to please Jaga. But when he understood what she and Irena wanted of him, he frowned.

## Jan Dobraczyński

Jan knew what would happen if the Germans came and picked up the urchins. *For heaven's sake! He did not need Irena or Jaga to explain it to him,* he thought crossly. Yes, he knew the penalty for leaving the ghetto was execution, and these children had been found on the Aryan side of the city. But it was also automatic execution for any gentile caught helping them. This was a harebrained scheme. He shook his head in frustration.

If there had just been one or two children, Jan told himself, he might have risked it. He implored Jaga to understand. It was impossible to authorize thirty-two undocumented orphans. The Nazis would find out; they had made him responsible for this operation. And he wasn't willing to ask the orphanage directors—old friends of his father and his family—to take such a risk.

When he made the telephone call, he told the German supervisor the truth. Yes, there were Jewish children. Dozens of them. When he set the receiver down, it was no surprise his hands were shaking. The Nazi was wicked. Even as Nazis went, he was wicked. He might still come and shoot them all dead in the street just for the hell of it. But Jan had done the best he could. In theory, they had come to an arrangement. It had not come cheaply. Jan would keep quiet about that part. But there were no free passes with the Germans. Jan had twenty-four hours. He would have to pull some strings, call the old doctor. Irena would be furious. They had to smuggle the children back *inside* the ghetto.

A few telephone lines in and out of the ghetto still worked in the winter of 1941 through 1942, though Jews were forbidden to use them. Jan asked his father to contact Dr. Korczak, the legendary Polish educator and child-rights activist and director of the crowded ghetto orphanage. If Jan could get the children back over the wall without the guards shooting them, would the doctor take the orphans? Dr. Korczak said he would. The ghetto didn't offer many choices either.

Now the hands of the clock seemed to hasten round their course. Word came of a breach in the wall in the Muranow district, unless the Germans had already closed it. No matter, there would be another. The ghetto orphans would know the best ways through.

Jan explained the deal to the social workers. Send children back into the ghetto? Irena was in and out of that wretched place three, four times daily. Jan's solution was nothing more than a slow death for the children in exchange for a Nazi bullet. Jan must be blind to what happened in the ghetto to agree to such a cowardly, pathetic plan. Jan reeled. Irena fumed. But their quarrel got them nowhere; Jan had already made his deal with the German inspector.

This stealth operation needed the small predawn hours, the cover of darkness, but after curfew, soldiers' orders were shoot to kill. The children must crawl back through breaks in the wall now, while the last anxious residents rushed for home, before the dangerous quiet. On the other side, Dr. Korczak assured Jan, someone from the orphanage would meet them. Jan escorted the children himself. His conscience nagged him. He could expect no sympathy from Irena. Her disgust was clear, and she'd refused to have anything to do with his plan.

The children edged nearer to Jan, hushed as they walked, their breath sending cloudy wisps into the cold air. In the snow, everything seemed louder, and Jan listened for a noise out of place, for the crunch of footsteps following them. His fingertips grew cold in his gloves; his head ached from long minutes on high alert. Jan's breath caught when a young boy's voice returned the code word through the wall.

Over there, on the other side, this was a children's enterprise! A scuffle sounded, a rattle, and then a passageway opened. The children made no hesitation. One by one, they smiled their tired good-byes and wriggled past him into that other world. A girl with a bright hair ribbon whispered brightly, *Good-bye, Mr. Dobraczyński.* A small boy stumbled in the outsized shoes flopping on his feet. Then went the cheeky pair of brothers he had no doubt would be back over the wall within days. He waited to hear their quiet landings. "A few minutes before curfew," Jan reported back, "each child went through, and disappeared from the official list of young beggars."

Irena checked on the children the next day at the ghetto orphanage, and the old doctor assured her they had made it safely. She tried to understand the logic of Jan's decision, but could only feel defeat. Irena cursed herself. She should have taken responsibility, figured out something herself. Never again would she sit by and allow this to happen. She'd work harder than ever to save as many of these innocent children as she could, and she would not tell Jan Dobraczyński a word.

## Escape Routes

By spring, desperate Jewish parents were trying to send their beloved but starving children across the wall. Sometimes whole families escaped and hid together. But parents had to go out, try to work, or somehow provide for themselves and their offspring. They could not evade the Gestapo for long. Caught in the wrong place at the wrong time, snagged in roundups, betrayed, or just unlucky, they were shot, or sent away. Some suffered shame and guilt for abandoning aged parents or helpless infants to the jaws of the ghetto. Everyone didn't have the physical or mental fitness to survive passage out. Stricken parents sent children who could walk out on their own, or with friends or strangers, even paid smugglers.

Wanda Ziemska was eight years old when she stepped into the murky waters. "Above the entrance to the sewer, I said good-bye to Father, who stayed behind," she remembered. "The journey through the sewers was quite complicated. At times it looked like a dirty river. . . . I can remember how hard it was for me to climb out of the sewer—I couldn't reach from one rung to another." Hundreds of children made the same frightening passage through the sewers.

Myriad routes led in and out of the Jewish Quarter. Twenty-two different gates guarded the ghetto, and smugglers came to know the sentries who could be bribed or distracted and even those who let contraband through out of goodwill. Schemers had long been throwing food and goods over the wall to lookouts on the other side. The wall could be scaled with people keeping watch on both sides. Mothers threw their babies over the wall, never knowing if anyone caught them and took them to safety.

Food and medicines passed through the gates in fire engines, ambulances, garbage carriers, horse-drawn carts, hearses, and trucks carrying official goods. Like Irena, certain people had legal passes to enter the gates—city workers, rent and tax collectors, electricians, managers and owners of Polish businesses and their Polish employees, and the priest who served the two Catholic churches inside the ghetto boundaries. Undertakers hid the smuggled goods in compartments in their coffins. Large-scale operations took advantage of ghetto boundaries that ran beside internal walls of buildings. Some were able to knock holes in the walls that separated the ghetto from the Aryan side and carefully concealing the openings. People might also escape or run contraband by jumping between rooftops.

The Warsaw court building on Leszno Street buzzed with trafficking. Though officially on the Aryan side, the ghetto entirely surrounded it. To enter from the Aryan side, one had to follow a narrow passage from Murkowski Place, along Biala Street to a back entrance. Poles and Jews mingled freely for court proceedings in the building, though Jews were required to wear their Star of David armbands. Dozens of boys and girls escaped through the courthouse, often guided by teenage girls. The janitor helped spirit children through back rooms and little used hallways to the other side.

Irena's best way to protect these children once they escaped was to give them a completely new identity. But the Germans wouldn't issue a *kennkarte* for any child that showed up at the office. These identity cards bore a serial number, a fingerprint as well as a name, address, and photograph. They required a file of documents proving the child's identity. Irena and her network scrounged for ways to come up with blank or forged birth certificates to use as the basis for these fake files. One of the simplest methods was also the saddest. When a Christian child died in an orphanage, the key was not to report the death. The name and registry number could create a new identity and safe place for a Jewish child. The chance to make a ghoulish swap like this required timing and patience.

Earlier, in the autumn, Irena and her network got a

lucky break. A church burned to the ground in the distant city of Lwów, and the parish priest offered to give them his remaining cache of blank birth certificates. Because the fire had destroyed all the church records, they could not be cross-checked by German authorities. Once Irena had a birth certificate, they could begin to produce all the papers the Germans required. Irka had made the dangerous journey to fetch them and carried them back on the train tucked in an old suitcase she tried to carry lightly. Lwów was about to have a birthrate explosion.

That winter, the women used a few of the precious blank documents to save an old friend, Dr. Witwicki and his family. They had been hiding and in constant danger since the Germans took over. The professor spent his time sculpting handmade dolls in a quiet room on Brzozowa Street in the Old Town, and Irena smuggled them into the ghetto. She had recently taken a stash of the dolls to the Jewish orphanage for the littlest of Jan Dobraczyński's street children. She still fretted about those thirty-two youngsters, and by now she knew all their names and faces.

Irena wanted to help her friends—Adam, Ewa, Rachela, Jozef, Ala—flee and go into hiding on the Aryan side, too. She would find them papers; she would find safe houses. She implored them all, *come now*. When they shook their heads sadly, Irena couldn't hide her frustration and worry.

*It's too risky to hide a Jew, Irena,* Ewa told her over and over. *Life was not so different now, not really,* Ewa insisted.

It's just the same as on the Aryan side, the same work as always. The children just need a little heart and a lot of bread. "Please don't ask me," she told Irena, squeezing her friend's hand kindly. "I won't stay with you—I can't endanger you like that."

Irena understood. She risked her life daily for the street children. She risked her life smuggling vaccinations into the ghetto. If her friends asked her to stay at home to avoid the danger, would she? No, she would not. So, instead, Irena and her friends on both sides of the wall threw themselves into their dangerous mission.

In the months to come, Irena and Irka smuggled more than a thousand doses of typhus vaccination into the walled quarter. Other friends and coworkers in her network—like Jaga Piotrowska and Jadwiga Deneka—smuggled in another five thousand. Irena carried wads of cash through the checkpoints rolled in her undergarments and medicines in her work bag with the false bottom. Throughout the Jewish Quarter people whispered her code name, Jolanta—the woman who could manage anything.

# 7

## Expanding Operations

*Out through the Sewer*

### Irka Schultz—Aryan Side, 1942

Irka Schultz walked away from the ghetto checkpoint letting go a great sigh of relief. She was lucky any afternoon when her heart did not ache for hours after passing through the gate and witnessing the guards' capricious cruelty. Somewhere in the distance a gunshot sounded. A dog barked. A tram jounced on the tracks. All part of the mix in occupied Warsaw. But when she heard the scrape and rattle of a manhole cover, Irka froze.

The noise came again, metal rubbing against metal, and the sniffling of a child. Irka glanced around, checking for anyone showing too much curiosity, then fell to her knees and peeled off her gloves. Gripping the iron plate, she heaved and it slid away. Again she scanned the street, her knees growing cold and her skirt damp from the dirty

78

ice where she knelt. Only a Jewish person in fear for his or her life would crawl down into the dark, cold muck. Irka leaned in to see who was there. The stench rose up and knocked her back. Gulping a breath and holding it, Irka looked again. A small child's face etched with fear and hunger gazed up with big eyes. The girl struggled, too small or too weak to climb the ladder. Irka grasped her under the arms and lifted her free, then hissed into the darkness. *Witaj! Czy jest tu ktoś? Hello! Is anyone there?*

There was no answer, and in one swift movement, Irka slid the cover back in place, took hold of the grimy little hand and stood. Filthy from her tightly combed-back hair to her scuffed little shoes, the girl was wet and shivering and about to break loose bawling. She was also starving, you could tell just by looking at her. They mustn't draw attention. Irka put a finger to her lips. *Shhh.* The child nodded, her eyes growing wider, her hand clenching two of Irka's fingers.

Irka stayed alert, watching for trouble. Anti-Semitic hooligans and petty blackmailers prowled the areas near the ghetto, looking for anyone who appeared desperate or famished enough to be Jewish. Jews on the Aryan side were always vulnerable to extortion.

Stay calm, Irka told herself. Walk slowly. Fear was the biggest tell. Parents sending their children out of the ghetto instructed them to wear the best disguise of all, a happy face. Irka looked down and modeled a big, bright smile to the girl, drawing her fingers up along her cheeks in a silent gesture. That's when she noticed the scrap of paper attached to the child's dress with a sewing needle, and her breath caught in her throat. On the paper was written a single digit—the child's age, she guessed. A mother's act of faith, her last plea for her daughter.

Irka led the girl toward the shadows of a side street and considered what to do. The child needed a doctor. Her skin was hot and her wrist too thin. Irka tried not to hold it too tightly. The orphanage on Nowogrodzka Street was the only place with physicians on staff. This wasn't the first time she had discovered a Jewish child on the wrong side of the wall. In fact, it happened with a depressing regularity. She would clean up the girl as best she could, and get word to Irena. Then Irka would pick up the telephone and ring the Father Boduen orphanage. She would speak in code to her friend there, Wladyslawa. This time, maybe she would ask, "Can I stop by *today* to drop off that coat I borrowed?" "Today" meant *emergency*.

She and Irena had already set up one of their first protocols in cooperation with the Father Boduen Catholic orphanage. It had stemmed from a crisis. Like Irena, Jaga, and Jadwiga, Irka was in and out of the ghetto several times a day. She had brought out a Jewish toddler, but they had not been able to secure documents for the little tyke. Every single one of the blank birth certificates from the priest in Lwów had been used, and they had no other source of forged identity papers. Irka and Irena had debated in hushed, urgent tones. Whom could they trust? Wladyslawa Marynowska?

The Father Boduen orphanage employed Wladyslawa, nicknamed Władka, as a senior housemother and social worker. Irka dithered. The woman was a longtime, trusted friend, but one did not draw friends lightly into this dangerous underworld, especially friends with a child of their own. Was it right to ask Władka to risk her own young son, Andrzej? If he were threatened, could Władka keep secrets?

The Gestapo suspected the orphanage might be harboring Jewish children, and Irka worried that a child without proper identification was too great a risk. The decision hung in the air between the women. They weighed its kind every day.

"You can be calm." Irena's voice was steady; she was sure of Władka Marynowska. Irka nodded and reached for her coat.

It was only a short walk from the social welfare office on Zlota Street to the orphanage. Irka walked briskly, still feeling nervous about approaching Władka. This toddler was one of "hers." It was hard not to feel protective.

Władka's job was to vet prospective foster parents, and she knew better than anyone how to find caregivers willing to take in children for the customary boarding fee the city offered.

When Irka reached the imposing brick building of the

orphanage and climbed the steps, she was still trying to figure out what she would say. Władka's warm greeting ended her agonizing. Irka asked, would Władka take a walk with her? Władka's wise eyes narrowed and she did not hesitate despite the probability of wet winter boots and frozen fingers. Certain conversations could not be overheard, for Father Boduen's likely harbored Gestapo spies.

Irka felt she could trust Władka, but the war made all sorts of decent people fainthearted. The women walked, their boots crunching on the snow, and Irka clung to this last moment of safety. Once she spoke, there was no turning back.

*There's a toddler. . . .* Irka faltered. *. . . Several children. They need homes, care.*

Władka brightened. *Of course, Irka, it is no problem. Just bring them to the office and—*

Irka took a deep breath and interrupted. *Władka, there are no papers.*

*There.*

*It was done.*

Only a fool could misunderstand the situation, and nothing about Władka Marynowska was foolish.

Irka marveled that her feet kept walking, that people passed by without a second glance, that the ground stayed solid beneath her in that instant when everything became fragile, so fragile, it could shatter as easily as a pane of ice slipping from a roof.

An undocumented child was almost certainly Jewish. Władka had her own child to think of, her little boy, Andrzej. Anyone who turned up at the orphanage, a wet nurse, a girl with child and desperate, a couple wanting to adopt, could be a Nazi spy. Why, an old friend might be an enemy operative in this terror-stricken occupied city.

Władka kicked a bit of melting ice with her boot and looked every direction but at Irka, and Irka knew her friend was calculating: Was Irka trustworthy? That was Władka's dilemma.

The two longtime friends locked eyes. Władka took a deep breath. *Yes, I will take the child.*

Irka Schultz let out a breath. *Thank you.*

They said no more.

Back at the steps of Father Boduen's, Władka told Irka, *Come back another time, and we can discuss how we make placements.*

Irka waved a cheery hand.

The next time Irka visited the orphanage, she brought along a woman she introduced to Władka as Sonia. "Sonia," as well as Ala, might sometimes deliver children, she said. Ala was able to slip in and out of the ghetto with the pass given her as chief nurse of the Jewish sector. Sonia was the code name used by a Polish nurse named Helena Szeszko, a senior operative in a resistance cell in the medical underground. Ala had worked with her for months, and now drew Helena into Irena's growing network.

Helena, too, had one of Dr. Juliusz Majkowski's epidemic control passes, and could come and go from the ghetto. She smuggled sick Jewish children and hidden supplies in municipal ambulances.

Władka knew none of this, for her own protection and for the safety of others in the network. Across the city, dozens of cells functioned in secrecy and isolation. A number of the people resisting the Germans worked in circles connected with one another. Sometimes they knew, and sometimes they didn't.

Władka never asked Irka for more information. "It was enough to know that [Irka] had to take the Jewish children out of the ghetto and put them in a safe place," she said.

The women established a code. One of them would ring Władka on the telephone at the Father Boduen Home. They'd engage in frivolous talk, chat idly about borrowing skirts or scarves, make dates for tea or checking on ailing mothers. They would set a day and time. Something would be said about color. Color and clothing would identify the child in question—now and later. Władka kept a meticulous log of the children's clothing and appearances, especially the ones who came to her without documents. How else, after the war, would their parents find them?

## You Can Only Die Once

Irena's heart ached for orphans trapped in the ghetto. When she found Jewish children hiding for their lives on the

Aryan side, she relied on her network to arrange homes for them. But orphans had no loving parents, no one with hope enough to send them out of the ghetto. And toddlers and babies could not flee alone. These children collected every day at her friends' youth circles, and no matter how hard they fought the hunger and disease, these ailments gained strength. Small bodies had only the breath of a chance.

Once it became clear to Irena that children could escape the ghetto, she felt bound to do everything in her power to help them. With her epidemic control pass, she could legally take a Jewish child with tuberculosis to a sanatorium in Otwock. If now and then a cough turned out not be tuberculosis, the child disappeared into a friend's home in their old village. If the Nazi's discovered Irena faking cases of tuberculosis, they'd likely shoot her. They would shoot her whether they caught her smuggling vaccinations or children. She would be just as dead for either kindness.

Irena did not want fear, even fear of death, to weigh heavily in her choices about how to live her life. She wanted to be like her papa. The winter she was six years old, a typhoid epidemic took hold in their village. The highly contagious disease swept through households, carrying off the young and the old and sometimes entire families. Irena had not been allowed to go to the homes of her friends, even before some of her playmates had died. But Papa carried on, as always, treating sick and infected patients, calling at homes no other doctor would visit.

A girl begging in the ghetto.
*Yad Vashem*

When Papa felt the first shakes and shivers, he knew he had caught the terrible fever. Soon, he was burning hot in the afternoons and whispering in wild delirium. The aunts fussed and fussed. No, Irena must not go near the sickroom. No, she could not see Papa. Everything would have to be disinfected. Irena and Mama would have to go stay with relatives. There wouldn't be any hugs and kisses to spoil Irena again until Papa was well. They didn't want Irena to catch the infection. It was too dangerous for a child.

Papa had struggled against the typhoid for weeks, and he did not get better. She remembered the day they told her Papa had died. It was five days before her seventh birthday

When Irena thought of the risks she took going in and out of the ghetto, she decided she might as well go all out. She could only die once.

By early spring, 1942, Irena and her cell ran a full-scale operation helping Jews "disappear" into the city. False documents gave Irena's little pretenders the higher degree of safety, and she continued to make strenuous efforts to get them. At the orphanage, healthy children with fair hair and blue eyes, or without common Jewish features, could be folded into the life of the orphanage once they had records and an official registry number. These "Polish"-looking children did not give Irena nightmares. What jolted her awake at night were dreams about the children with "bad" Semitic features.

Irena's fears sprang from very real danger. The network could not allow these children to be seen for an instant on the Aryan side. They arrived at the orphanage in burlap sacks slung over a workman's shoulders, delivered to the back door as laundry or potatoes. Władka had to locate a foster family ready to spirit the children away and keep them constantly quiet and hidden. These youngsters spent no more than a few hours at the Father Boduen Home. As the numbers of children increased in the spring of 1942, Jaga Piotrowska and Jadwiga Deneka joined the women transporting them.

The children had to summon as much courage as those smuggling them. Ala came from a famous theatrical family. She coached children at playing sick in order to save them. More often, though, on their perilous ambulance rides with hidden children, Ala and Helena counted on the Nazi fear of infection and simply hid the youngster under piles of dirty rags or inside already occupied coffins.

Older children with especially "good looks" who could learn Catholic prayers and were fearless actors could flee the ghetto by walking out the front door of a Catholic church that straddled the ghetto line. Stopped by the German sentries, their lives depended upon how well they could speak Polish and recite their catechism. Others might be smuggled through tunnels dug in the church's crypts and basements, a route used to run contraband medical supplies into the ghetto. The most inventive methods, though, involved simply leaving the ghetto with small children in sacks, suitcases, and toolboxes. One boy escaped that spring by tucking his feet into the back of a man's boots and walking with him across the check point hidden underneath his overcoat.

Helena Szeszko specialized in counterfeit documents as well as medical care. She and her husband, Leon, had started in the underground by setting up a cell to forge identity papers. By June, Leon had become a smuggler as well. He was a tram engineer and his route ran through the walled Jewish district. On the first run of the morning, when the trams sat empty on the ghetto side, babies were tucked into "forgotten" bags under a seat or in the back of a compartment. Sleeping infants fit snugly inside briefcases.

Someone had to brave the streets of the ghetto before curfew to make the drop-off in the empty railyard. A handful of people had permission to break curfew, and Ala was one of them, due to her duties as chief nurse. She also had the experience needed to administer just the right dose of sedative to a tiny body. Then the tram rolled along its route to the Aryan side, and at the first stop Irena or Jaga would board, with all the calm they could muster, and surreptitiously collect the package.

When Irena's operatives could not find safe homes in time, the women had no choice but to take desperate chances and keep them in their own homes until a place was found for them. Irena, Jaga, Jadwiga, and Władka all hid children in their apartments at times. At Władka's, her elementary-school-aged son, Andrzej, had the grave responsibility of helping his mother care for desperately ill younger children, leading them to the bathroom and helping them.

As Irena's network grew, so did the surveillance. The children came and went from the Father Boduen Home, and with every passing day the Gestapo grew more suspicious. German agents combed Władka's official records, searching for any scrap of evidence. But the real records were never in the file cabinets. Władka would never be so foolish. When the paperwork frustrated them, the Gestapo held guns to people's heads in the corridor and bullied all the staff with threats of mass executions.

The Nazis scrutinized the paperwork of "orphans" arriving officially with such tenacity that Irena decided more of the children would have to sift through her system off the record. Irena commanded a growing citizen's army, which now included nearly two-dozen people, drawn together from the political underground, the welfare offices, and the Jewish community. Such a network could not go about business without the Gestapo catching a whiff of the activity. They were on the hunt. The greater number of people Irena involved, the greater the chance someone would slip.

# 8

## Rumors

**Summer 1942**

People who'd survived the winter and seen spring come to the Jewish Quarter may have believed they had seen the very depths of human suffering. But in the first half of 1942, monstrous rumors reached tentacles into the ghetto.

The whispers were said to have started with a Jewish man who'd escaped from a camp in the east near the village of Chelmno. Szlama Ber Winer said he'd seen a Nazi killing operation murdering thousands of Jews. SS men had gassed groups of them in a long container. "It looked like a normal large [truck], in gray paint, with two hermetically closed rear doors." The man said the Nazis ordered him to help bury sixteen hundred Jews gassed at the camp in roughly two weeks. His parents and siblings had been among the dead.

No one wanted to believe such stories, and they sparked much debate. Possibly, they were exaggerated. Some tales proved untrue, so which could be believed? Everyone knew of Jews sent to labor camps, but large numbers of Poles had also been forced to work for the Germans. In Vilna, forty thousand Jews had been killed, but ten thousand had survived. Reports the Nazis had deported large numbers of Jews from other Polish cities could be explained by other rumors that Jews were being resettled in the east of occupied Poland.

No one had been deported from the Warsaw ghetto. Some people argued the Nazis planned to concentrate the Jewish people in large groups to more easily control them and exploit their labor. Though brutal, this could be seen as rational. Some educated, wealthy Jews believed the Germans might destroy rural and small town Jews, but would not dare wipe out the Jewish community in Warsaw, the heart of Jewry in Europe.

Those who did believe the horror stories became desperate to get their children over, under, or through the wall. Irena and her friends' work helping these boys and girls to safety took the time and energy of a full time job. Many more youngsters might be saved if they had a better system to shelter them. Getting them out of the ghetto was easier than keeping them safe in the Aryan sector.

Irena needed a more fail-proof way to send Jewish children to Catholic orphanages, and to place them with willing foster families. They must move more children, more quickly. Irena realized that she must recruit someone higher up the chain in the children's welfare department. One person had the power to make this happen. Irena needed the help of Jan Dobraczyński.

Jaga tried to remind Irena that she was wrong in her judgment of Jan. Jan was guided by his strong Catholic faith, and he did not lack a moral compass, even if he and Irena could not agree on which direction true north rested. Jaga's face said to Irena that she was being narrow-minded and stubborn. *We need his help,* Jaga told her gently.

Still, Irena resisted. She could not forget those thirty-two boys and girls Jan had sentenced to the ghetto. But she had no other ideas. She called a meeting of women in his division, about a half dozen who were already involved up to their necks. With Jaga at the lead and Irena right behind, they marched into Jan's office.

Irena had no evidence Jan actively aided the enemy, but he was friendly with the Germans who oversaw his department. Sometimes that was a fine line. Poles who collaborated with the Nazis risked censure, or worse, from Polish resistance. The underground government ruled a widespread, well-organized, and fearless opposition to the Nazi invaders, including a secret justice system that held trials and passed down sentences on people who collaborated with the Germans. Secret agents carried out death sentences without mercy. This was a dangerous time to refuse to help people like Irena. Or was it more dangerous to get involved?

Jan listened as Jaga explained they'd come to ask his help. He could use his authority and contacts, not only with the Sisters at Father Boduen's, but with orphanages all across Poland. He could find reliable people to help hide the children. Jan agreed to do what he could. Irena did not know he aided the resistance factions on the political right, but she could guess that his patriotism could not be questioned. Her discomfort came from Jan's uncertain ideas about Jews. She couldn't know that Jan remembered the children he had returned to the ghetto, too, or that his conscience troubled him and that his strong faith was calling him to protect the innocent.

Jan followed through on the promise quickly, reaching contacts in the resistance who agreed to guide Jewish children to convents and orphanages. He made a standing arrangement with the nuns who ran the homes. When Irena and her network needed to transfer a Jewish child secretly, he would sign the request. Normally, the section manager would not sign these papers, but Jan's signature became a code identifying a child requiring special care.

Ala became the one in Irena's network who contacted Jan and coordinated advance logistics with the Catholic charities when a ghetto child needed saving. So far, she had resisted taking out her own six-year-old daughter, Rami, as she couldn't bear to part with her. She knew she couldn't wait any longer.

Ala worried her ghetto pass would soon be worthless. Rumors swirled of coming deportations. Irena begged her to act quickly to save both herself and Rami. Ala wouldn't leave, but she agreed at last to part with her daughter.

Ala took Rami with her to visit Róża Zawadzka, at whose apartment she regularly delivered the little one she spirited away from the ghetto. Rami had visited Róża before with her mother so, at first, nothing seemed unusual. Ala and Róża talked in quiet voices for a long while, and then, when it was time to go, Ala kissed Rami gently and left the apartment.

At first Irena shuttled Ala's little girl from one orphanage to another, but Rami was one of the difficult children to place. She did not look like what a German thought of as Polish. Róża and Irena finally found a Polish aristocrat couple active in the underground, who agreed to take Rami into their family.

With her system streamlined, Irena turned to another nagging worry. Once the war was over, how would parents find their children, these many children disappearing through her machinations? Only this small handful of conspirators knew the children's real names, the identities they shed like dirty clothes. Only Irena, as the leader, knew how all the pieces of the puzzle fit together. If something happened to her, the Jewish children would vanish almost as surely as if they had perished.

## The Ask—July 1942

Twenty-two-year-old Henia Koppel's only child was born in the ghetto. Despite the cruel conditions, she had been able to give her daughter, baby Elżbieta, everything she needed to thrive. Henia's husband, Josel, had been a rich banker, and her father, Aron Rochman, a successful businessman. With foresight, Josel stashed away much of the family fortune in a secret numbered bank account in Switzerland, one of Europe's neutral countries that the Nazis had not invaded. In early summer of 1942, the couple still had enough money that Henia could hope baby Bieta, as they called her, would have a future.

But those rumors! Warnings! Jews who had escaped Lublin and Równo reported the Germans had killed or deported every Jewish person they could round up, that in some other cities they were deporting Jews at the rate of one thousand a day. Bieta's family and many others in the ghetto believed the only possible way to stay alive was to work for the Germans. There was some small comfort in the story, whispered ear to ear, that a wave of deportations at the Łódź ghetto had only taken the feeble, disabled, sick, and starving. Those unfit to "work to live" were targeted, not the strong and the sturdy.

Since the beginning of the occupation, people working for the Germans in Warsaw had not been so readily shipped off to labor camps. They had special work permits allowing them leave the ghetto to go to their jobs. They didn't get paid for the work and received barely enough food to keep from starving to death, but it seemed the Germans were happy to keep them around.

As spring warmed to summer, those work permits became more valuable than gold. By July, the pieces of papers were selling for five thousand zlotys. (Close to fifteen thousand in today's dollars.)

Henia's husband, Jozel, had enough cash saved to buy his wife one of the precious permits that got her a job at a factory in the ghetto. Walter Toebbens operated a number of manufacturing plants with Jews as slave labor. The factory at number 44 Nowolipie Street had three thousand workers producing shoes and other leather goods, wool sweaters, and socks for the army. Other shops manufactured textiles and furs, did carpentry and metalwork. Henia took a much coveted spot as a seamstress. But Toebbens's managers didn't let mothers bring children with them during the long hours they labored at the factory. Bieta was six months old and breastfeeding. Henia could not leave her baby. Even the family's money could not solve this problem.

As ever, Irena and Ala had their ears tuned to families in desperate circumstances. Ala knew the factory manager, Walter Toebbens, and she had tried to get him to change his policy about nursing mothers. Irena and Ewa Rechtman had smuggled Elżbieta's older cousin to the Aryan side and found a foster family to care for her. There were already connections between the family and Irena's network. Now, Irena believed she could help Henia keep Bieta safe, too. Driven by her conviction that the Nazis were bent on killing every Jewish child in the ghetto, Irena made a bold proposal to the Koppel family. Give beloved Bieta to a stranger? It was unthinkable. She'd be well-cared for, Irena assured the parents and grandparents.

*But can you guarantee she'll be safe?* No. That was not a promise Irena, nor anyone, could make in wartime Poland. She couldn't even promise that she and Bieta would make it out of the ghetto that day. But Irena vowed she would risk her life trying. Being honest, she had to admit that if she and the baby were discovered at the checkpoint, they'd both be shot. But wasn't it true, they might even be shot at random on the doorstep leaving the apartment?

Jozel was a clear-sighted man. He knew if his daughter stayed in the ghetto, she would die. Maybe not soon, but . . . The best thing they could do for Bieta was to hand her over to this uninvited, insistent stranger. Henia agreed. Bieta had fallen asleep in her mother's arms. Henia held her close to her heart and breathed the sweet, milky scent of her infant. Tears ran down her face. Everyone in the room felt their heart breaking. But Irena told the parents and Bieta's grandfather they must act quickly. Soon, it would be too late.

Irena reached out and took the infant. Henia's green

eyes pleaded with her. *There must be another way.* Irena's eyes welled with tears as she held the mother's gaze for a long moment. Henia patted Bieta with a gentle hand, then a bit more firmly. The infant did not wake. It was good. Irena placed her hand on the small chest to make sure Bieta's breath was not too shallow. She nodded. The tranquilizer was working.

Irena would send word as soon as they made it out safely. And, yes, she assured Henia, no matter what, the silver baby spoon, engraved with the child's birth date, would never leave Elżbieta's side.

It was time to go. Irena would once more risk her life and the life of a child's passing through the gates, past the Nazi guards. She'd passed between the sentries too many times to count, but no number would increase her chance of surviving this time.

A builder, Henryk, had agreed to hazard this crossing with her. He opened his wooden toolbox, and they laid six-month-old Bieta inside, tucking the blanket firmly around her, checking that nothing blocked the little girl's air holes. They dropped the lid with care. The hasp clicked into place.

Out on the street, Henryk stored the box on the flat-bed of his truck among the piles of bricks. His contractor's work pass let Henryk come in and out of the ghetto, making him another valuable part of Irena's network. He gave Irena a quick, tense smile. He had only to drive the truck through the gate, past the armed guards and a short distance to his stepmother's home. The midwife, Stanislawa Bussold, was one of Irena's "emergency room" operatives.

Irena climbed into the passenger's seat, the old clutch lurching as Henryk stepped on the gas. She stole a swift look back at their cargo, praying that no bricks had shifted or fallen. They drove in silence toward Nalewki, once flourishing with businesses and affluent apartments, now lined with shuttered shops, closed bakeries, rusting street signs, and piles of garbage. Now, there was a gate there, and they would have to pass through it to save baby Bieta.

Getting through the checkpoint was the most dangerous few moments of any day. Irena and Henryk joined the line of vehicles, long this afternoon, her nerves tightening, minutes ticking by, her hands growing cold with sweat, slippery on the door handle. There was no turning back now. There had never been.

At last, a soldier gestured them forward, and Henryk gave over their ghetto passes with cool self-possession that impressed Irena. The guard looked hard at her, then at Henryk.

*What's in the back?* His eyes narrowed. This time Henryk stumbled, answering.

*Raus! Out!*

Irena's pulse leapt. Surely, they could see it throbbing at her throat. Today, they would not get the baby through after all. Henryk stepped from the truck, moved to the back as he was ordered. Irena stilled herself. She must not look around at the noise, canvas flapping, bricks scraping against bricks, clattering, knocking and poking. It was an effort not to squirm. And then, Henryk opened the door, got in beside her, and the guards waved them through the gates.

Neither said a word for some time. The truck slowed at a corner and Irena grasped Henryk's arm, smiled at him in relief. *Are you fine the rest of the way alone, Henryk? It will look better.* He nodded. Irena slid from the seat and waved to Henryk as he drove away. She turned in the other direction. Irena knew that, if anyone were being watched, she was the danger to this mission. Maybe Henryk guessed that his stepmother sometimes helped Jewish women deliver their babies in secret. He certainly knew her home served as a critical stopover for Jewish children. In their first hours and days outside the ghetto, someone had to clean the smuggled children, feed them, and get them medical attention. After months of near starvation, their need for a doctor's care was often urgent.

If they had "bad looks," they would need makeovers to lighten their hair color. Sometimes baby Jewish boys transformed into Polish girls to hide their circumcision. If the children were old enough, the emergency room guardians would teach them their Catholic prayers and to speak Polish. Catechism drills were a favorite Nazi "test" to catch out Jews. Knowing Catholic prayers by heart had become a basic tool of wartime survival. In their first weeks on the Aryan side, every hint of a child's Jewish identity was erased.

A few days after baby Bieta made her toolbox journey to the Aryan side, the Nazis confirmed the rumors that the Jews would be deported. They would leave by train for resettlement to the east.

# 9

## Deportation

### First *Aktion*—July 22, 1942

While Irena's network routed children over and under and through the wall, some two thousand Jewish children remained locked in a prison within a prison. Most of these youngsters had been incarcerated when police caught them smuggling food. The chief of the Judenräte, Adam Czerniakow, had been negotiating with the German *Kommisar* of the ghetto, hoping to get these children released. They weren't criminals. They were hungry and they certainly hadn't hurt anyone by bringing food into the ghetto. Czerniakow knew that often child smugglers were feeding entire families.

Czerniakow had also been asking the *Kommisar* and other Nazi officials for some word about what was really coming down concerning all the scuttlebutt. Deportation . . . resettlement . . . labor camps . . . He needed something to tell his people. The *Kommisar* told him each time he asked that he'd heard nothing of the sort and that he would ask and let Czerniakow know.

Another important man in the ghetto, and a friend of Irena's, Dr. Janusz Korczak had no expectation of any assurance from the Germans. He did all he could for the children he loved, his two hundred, give or take, orphans, trying to bring them some joy each day. It was late, and he was awake in his small room at number 16 Sienna Street, writing. He had been gripped all day with a grim sense of foreboding. The doctor was in his early sixties, and the following day, July 22, 1942, was his birthday. He had endured the trials in his life, stood up for what he believed, and now he was a skinny old man, bald and stooped, and he was tired.

Dr. Korczak had no illusions about the Nazis.

Turning to his journal, he poured out his thoughts and longings onto the paper. "It is a difficult thing," he wrote, "to be born and to learn to live. What remains for me is a much easier task: to die. . . . I do not know what I would say to the children as a farewell. I would want to say so much. . . . [It is] ten o'clock. Shots: two, several, two, one, several. Perhaps my window is poorly darkened right now. But I will not interrupt my writing. The opposite: my thoughts take flight (a single shot)."

The next morning, on her way to work, Irena heard the whispers of trouble. Something was happening in the

Janusz Korczak with several orphans in his institution.
*Yad Vashem*

Jewish Quarter. Extra soldiers stationed at the checkpoints; some had been seen on nearby rooftops. A pang of dread settled in her heart. It could not be good. All news in the ghetto these days was bad news.

A summer rain splashed the streets by the time Irena managed to get to the Jewish Quarter. Rain could not thin the crowds in the streets like this. People clumped together on the sidewalk where a sign was posted. Thick with black words on white paper, the notice on the wall began:

### All Jews living in Warsaw

irrespective of sex or age will be deported to the east.

So it was really happening! It was awful. Irena's contacts in the underground had told her the Nazi promises to resettle the Jews were lies. And now her friends were in danger for their lives! She wanted to run and find them and do whatever she could to keep them safe. The announcement had another twist to it, though. It went on to list people excluded from the deportation: people employed by the authorities or in German enterprises, people working in German-owned factories, members of the Jewish police, hospital staffs. . . . *Ala would be safe for now.* Sanitation squads, families, wives, and children of these people would also be exempt. Those people hospitalized in the ghetto hospital on the day of the evacuation and not in a condition to be moved, also exempt.

Each Jew evacuated could bring along up to fifteen kilograms (thirty pounds) of personal belongings, gold, jewelry, cash, and so forth. Irena wanted to believe that this meant the Germans did not plan to send the Jews to their death, but the cold that gripped her heart revealed that she knew the truth.

Irena walked as fast as she could without catching the attention of the soldiers, who were everywhere. She had to find her friends. Irena burst into the medical clinic where she often found Ala at this time of day. She wasn't there. They didn't know where she was. Irena tried to find her at home. Ala wasn't there either.

Irena headed back to make the rounds of the youth centers. Surely, she'd find her friends. Her dear friend Adam Celnikier had battled his way through despair by working in a center with young people, and she found him there now. He had stopped saying life in the ghetto wasn't worth living. The children had given Ewa a reason to live, too.

Irena's friends wouldn't likely be caught up in future roundups. Irena and Adam believed only the old and the very young would be resettled, those not capable of working. With a tired smile, Adam flexed an arm muscle. *See, I'm young and tough.* The gesture made her smile. Adam had a job, and a job meant safety. Rachela, Ewa, Jozef, and Ala were safe then, too.

Eventually, Irena had to head back to the Aryan side. Walking to the checkpoint, she heard the haggling. *Oszuści!*

The swindlers wasted no time. The price of work permits rose faster than people could pull money from their pockets. A divide towered between the fortunate and the unfortunate. Anyone without a work permit—the weak, the infirm, the half starved, the elderly, and all the children—were destined for the rail cars.

Once the children were gone, though, there'd be no need for youth centers. . . . Didn't that mean that her friends' jobs would disappear eventually? Irena would talk to her friends again about escaping the ghetto, and she'd increase her efforts to smuggle out the children. She must focus on the children she could save. She would have to hurry.

## The Good Fairy of the *Umschlagplatz*—July 1942

The next morning Irena arrived in the Jewish Quarter to hear the Nazis had ordered ten thousand Jews shipped east that day, after six thousand already yesterday. She went looking for her friends again. Someone had seen Ala that morning. Someone else had heard Ala had gone to the *Umschlagplatz*.

Racing north toward the railyard, frantic with worry, Irena did not let herself think the worst. Reaching the loading area, she tried to catch her breath, but could hardly keep from gagging. Thousands of bodies pressed together inside the *pen*—there was no other word for it. Guards stood outside the barbed wire that fenced the square,

Jews from the Warsaw ghetto boarding trains at the *Umschlagplatz* during the deportations, 1942. *Instytut Pamieci Narodowej United States Holocaust Memorial Museum, courtesy of Jerzy Tomaszewski*

threatening the pulsing throng. Soldiers holding their guns at the ready goaded new arrivals toward the railway platform and the holding area.

Irena searched the crowd, the stink of excrement and sweat drifting in the baking heat. No facilities. No shade. Even animals would be given water to drink. Irena felt faint, her focus hurtled across the writhing sea of bodies, looking for Ala's face, her springy black hair. She would never find her among all the faces, and what if she did? What then? Irena turned away, her chest heaving, hands shaking, helplessness overwhelming her.

At the last moment, as she gave in and started to walk away, a sudden commotion caught her eye, a flash of white. Ala's nurse uniform? On tiptoe, she strained to see. There. Her friend. It had to be. Irena dashed around the corner of the enclosure and stopped midstride. At the edge of the *Umschlagplatz*, just outside the wire boundary, a makeshift medical clinic buzzed with nurses and doctors. She spotted Ala. Fierce, strong Ala, with a fighter's spirit and poet's soul.

With great relief, Irena made her way to her friend. Standing next to Ala was a tall, dark-haired man named Nachum Remba, a longtime friend of Ala's family. He had a scheme, and Ala was helping him. Nachum wasn't a doctor but a clerk in the Judenräte and well connected with the Jewish resistance. *If the Germans truly planned to resettle the Jews,* Nachum said, *it would not do to send the frail and sick on a journey in crowded rail cars. There should be a clinic at the platform to care for those too weak to travel.*

It did not begin as a ruse, Ala explained to Irena. But, in the end, one had to fight fire with fire. Nachum had seen how distraught Ala was seeing people hounded to the *Umschlagplatz* and tried to get her to smile. *We'll need to perform some brilliant acting.* They both came from famous theatrical families in Warsaw. Together they rounded up some real doctors and nurses and set up a medical tent and dispensary on the outside corner of the *Umschlagplatz* plaza.

Ala and Nachum pretended they had permission to set up the clinic. They moved in gurneys and medical supplies and took over an area near the loading platform, a space lodged up against barbed wire, and opened for business. They identified anyone too weak or too young to travel and insisted on treatment and sometimes transfer to a hospital. All yesterday and today Ala and the others played along with the German ruse, insisting only the strong and able should resettle now. The Germans kept up their facade, playing along with these deluded Jewish doctors and nurses who had no way of knowing what happened to people at the other end of the line.

Nachum was a great actor! He was already well-known at the *Umschlagplatz* as the chief doctor of the ghetto—with the aid of some well-placed bribes, a doctor's white coat and his chutzpah, Nachum remained unchallenged by the Germans. He and Ala commandeered a hospital ambulance and started loading up adults and children.

## Jonas Turkow

Soldiers and Jewish policemen had been grabbing people and bullying them along toward the barbed-wire corrals, and Jonas, caught up in the crowd, had not been able to get away. In the midst of the noise and confusion, Nachum appeared, tall, confident, and smiling. *This one is too sick to make the difficult journey east,* he said, pointing and shrugging, as if it were of no particular interest. *What can I do?* his look said to the Nazi. Anyone else who approached a German in this manner would be shot. Jonas had seen it. On the loading docks, a bullet was the answer to any and every Jewish question. Nachum didn't ask questions. He gave orders. And one of his orders sent Jonas to the medical tent.

Inside the infirmary, the nurse ordered Jonas and the other "sick patients" to bed. She kept busy putting on rolls of fresh, white bandages. Jonas thought he might be dreaming. Maybe he was already dead? Nurses and doctors hustled from patient to patient with soothing attention, but when a German appeared at the door, Jonas knew he was still in the ghetto. The hush of the clinic disappeared, and the pace grew frenetic. He lay silent and still, and made himself small. At last, at some signal, the doors to the clinic shut, and ambulances rolled up to take them away. Jonas had to pass by the aloof SS men, who could point a finger and send him back out to board the train. He really did feel sick. Until the ambulance door closed behind him and drove away.

## Ala Gołab-Grynberg

Sometimes, Ala confessed, if someone looked too healthy even for good acting, the nurses took turns breaking people's legs in order to convince the Germans they were unfit for travel. In those cases, screams of pain did not need to be faked. Ala held their hands and murmured, but she could not spare her precious sedatives. Those she saved for fussy and frightened children, unable to feign illness, because the guards treated the infants the most harshly. They did not hesitate to dash babies to the ground or against railway cars in front of their weeping mothers. So Ala tucked the littlest ones under her oversized white coat and sauntered out past the sentries, cradling them under her armpit.

The people who passed scrutiny with the SS were loaded into ambulances and taken to one of the ghetto clinics, safe, at least one more day. The medical team and sanitation squads on the other end of those ambulance rides—Irka Schultz, Helena Szeszko, Jadwiga Deneka, and Irena Sendler—found ways to smuggle out a lucky few children.

Ala and Nachum's wild ruse continued, and Irena came

SS soldiers dragging a Jew in the street during an Aktion in the ghetto.
*Yad Vashem*

each day to the ghetto to do everything she and her network could to help get children out of the doomed quarter. On the loading platforms mothers tried to pass their children to Ala, whom everyone called "the good fairy." Ala and Nachum kept up their desperate efforts sixteen hours a day at the platforms, as thousands of people were forced onto the trains. Their efforts to save the weakest and most vulnerable became a race to save anyone possible. By the end of July, everyone understood. With the Nazis deporting ten thousand Jews a day, no one was safe.

The stomps and shouts of policemen echoed through the ghetto neighborhoods each morning. The searches started at 8 a.m. Most people stayed out of sight in their apartments. They had not thought the scenes on the street could grow more brutal, but when the ten thousand daily quota came up short, the police were relentless and vicious. They cordoned off streets, emptied buildings at gunpoint, and herded stricken residents under armed guard to the depot.

Those who argued or resisted lay scattered on the sidewalks—shot dead. At first, work papers saved people, and the lucky waved them like magic charms. The arbitrary *Selektions* increased the Jews' confusion and fear. One SS officer would look at people's papers and stamp them, the next day he would completely ignore the papers. Another officer seemed to decide people's fate on a whim or his mood. But growing pressure to get ten thousand bodies a day soon stripped any pass or permit of its power.

One afternoon, Irena found her friend Rachela alive but stricken, crazy with grief. She had left her daughter and her extended family at home for a few hours that morning to run errands for her youth circle. When Rachela returned, they were all gone. Broken suitcases and household belongings strewed the pavement, next to the corpses of neighbors too weak or too impertinent for the railroad trip. Shortly after Rachela had left the block, the police had arrived and cordoned off her street in a surprise *Selektion*.

Rachela's loss unhinged her, her sorrow intensified by the fact that now that her child was gone, she had a better chance of survival. Irena had seen how the children wandered about, neglected among the masses when police made their *Selektions*, while any mother with small children was grabbed automatically. Even children understood this. Some tried to run away from their mothers in order to save them.

Rachela's friends saw her unraveling, and unraveling was dangerous, a quick way to get selected. If she continued working at the youth center, and saw more deportations each day, Rachela would not survive. Some of Rachela's friends pulled strings to get her assigned to a labor gang. Now, Rachela would leave the ghetto every day to work in a German factory. She would be gone from reminders of the family she lost.

But, not much later, Irena discovered that Rachela and her work gang had disappeared. She searched and made inquiries, but could find no trace of her friend. Irena was heartbroken, but she understood how grief and loss might have stolen Rachela's will to live.

## The Lists

Until the *Aktion*, despite huge efforts at the risk of their lives, Irena and the women in the welfare office had hidden only a couple hundred Jewish children. Irena kept a list, calling it a card file, when in actuality is was a list of names and addresses, scrawled in code in a stubby hand on flimsy bits of cigarette paper and rolled up tightly for safe keeping.

In the beginning, all the women in her network kept these lists. Jaga and Wladyslawa, especially, each saw dozens of children come and go. Later, to reduce the security risks to the children and their guardians, Irena gathered them together into one place. But the real card file—the complete one—was lodged away, firmly, in Irena's mind. Although dozens of friends could fill in pieces, Irena was the only one who knew the big picture and the small details.

As the deportations continued, Irena's network grew. The numbers of children smuggled to the Aryan side also grew, which meant that the names in Irena's head multiplied. Irena realized that keeping track of the children in this haphazard fashion was not enough. But anything written on paper became evidence that could be used against you, and information about the children could be used to find them. And if they were found, everything would be undone. Irena had to figure out what to do with the lists.

Irena had no illusions. The number of children she could save seemed but a thimbleful in view of the thousands she saw taken to the *Umschlagplatz*. Still, each life mattered.

## Piotr Zysman

After four-year-old Piotr Zysman crawled from the sewers, he spent his first night outside the ghetto in Irena's apartment. Irena believed his parents, Jozef and Theodora, had made the right decision, but that did not make it any easier.

"Make sure he grows up to be a good Pole and an honorable man," Jozef had told her. He and Theodora knew they most likely would not live to see Piotr, their only son, again. Irena could not tell them any different. With ten thousand Jews shipped from the ghetto every day, it would not be long before there was no one left. Piotr had "good looks," like he might belong in a blond-haired Aryan family. His parents had to give him this chance. It would be a miracle if they survived.

A Polish couple named Waclaw and Irena Szyszkowski—friends of Jozef and Theodora—had agreed to take Piotr to live with them and their three small children. Waclaw and

Jozef had been law students together before the war. He was a big-boned, jolly-looking man, with a shock of blond hair. Waclaw worried about the danger to his children, but he could not refuse his friend Jozef this favor.

Piotr did not go straight to the Szyszkowski home once he climbed from the sewer. That night he went to Irena's apartment and she began to teach him everything he needed to learn to be safe on the Aryan side of Warsaw.

Piotr learned Catholic prayers and his new Polish name. *Never talk about your mama or papa*, Irena told him. *Piotr, you must always say that your house was bombed. Remember, never say you are Jewish.* It was a wretched thing to teach a child to recite, but Irena knew there was no choice. When the time came, a rendezvous was set and a liaison passed the little boy into the kind care of Waclaw and Irena Szyszkowski.

They treated Piotr like their own. But Waclaw soon realized adding another child to his family was more difficult than they had imagined. The neighbors grew nosy and suspicious. Over cake and coffee, with sideways glances and whispers, a neighbor hinted to Waclaw's wife that they knew the child she was hiding was Jewish. Waclaw got word to Irena. The Gestapo might come at any moment, so Piotr had to be moved instantly.

But Irena had not planned another place for him to go. She could not bring Piotr home as she suspected the SS was watching her apartment. Piotr was moved from one safe house to another for several weeks. This often happened and was difficult for the children. One little boy, in despair, begged Irena: *Please, how many mothers can you have? I am on my third already.*

In time, Piotr, like many of the children on Irena's lists, disappeared into one of the Catholic orphanages in her network.

## Treblinka 1941–1942

Seventy miles northeast of Warsaw, less than half a day's train ride, Jewish and Polish prisoners labored in a camp in a small village near the Bug River. A few miles away was the railway junction at Małkinia, and in the winter of 1941 the prisoners there worked in gravel pits, surrounded by forests.

In April of 1942, prisoners were assigned to work on a new construction project. There was a branch spur of rail line built from Małkinia junction, just a little jig-jag of a track, and long trenches were dug out. Workers from nearby villages were brought in to quickly set up barracks. The guards overseeing the camp were cruel and executed daily a couple of dozen Jewish workers. The field was covered with the dead, left for the dogs in the evening.

On June 15, 1942, the new project was at last completed—a camp for Jews. It was hidden from outside prying eyes by branches woven into barbed-wire fence surrounding the camp, and trees planted on the perimeter.

Watchtowers marked its four corners. The centerpiece of the camp was a long brick and concrete building. "The S.S. men," recalled Jan Sulkowski, a Polish prisoner forced to work on the building, "said it was to be a bath. . . . A specialist from Berlin came to put tiles inside and he told me that he had already built such chambers elsewhere."

The place looked clean and inviting. There were cloakrooms for undressing, with hooks for clothing and storerooms and a cashier's post for storing valuables, and piles of soap and towels. Tickets would be required of everyone entering the baths, and the price would be twenty zlotys.

Later, there would be a Red Cross camp infirmary, with a bright white and red banner, where those too infirm or troublesome to make the walk to the baths could receive special, faster treatment. The make-believe train depot, with the posted times of imaginary arrivals and departures, would be built months later, too, once word of the terrible truth had made its way back to Warsaw.

On July 23, 1942, when the camp received its first Jews from the ghetto, there was simply a railway platform to greet arrivals at the death camp in Treblinka. A flag waved over the roof when the gas chambers were running. There was a sign on the platform, in German and Polish:

### Jews of Warsaw, for your attention!

You are in a transit camp from which you will be sent
to a labor camp.

As a safeguard against epidemics you must immediately hand over your clothing and parcels for disinfection. Gold, silver, foreign currency, and jewelry must be placed with the cashier, in exchange for a receipt. These will be returned to you at a later time upon presentation of the receipt. For bodily washing before continuing with the journey all arrivals must attend the bathhouse.

In time, an orchestra would play Yiddish songs and cheerful camp marches, to cover the sound of barking dogs and people's screams.

# 10

## *Selektions*

### Dr. Korczak's Orphans—August 1942

Irena's daily routine took her to the ghetto in the afternoons when she had finished her social service job. But on August 6, she happened to come earlier and soon heard the latest rumor running through the Jewish Quarter. Dr. Korczak's orphanage would be targeted today. The children would all be deported.

Irena raced toward Sienna Street, hoping get there in time to warn the doctor or do something to help. Among the doctor's orphans were the thirty-two boys and girls that, less than a year ago, Jan Dobraczyński had returned through a chink in the wall. Irena thought of them as her children, and when she stopped in at the orphanage, the children shrieked with pleasure her at silly antics and the small gifts she brought them. They easily convinced her to stay and watch the fun they had playacting.

Irena spied the children at the corner of Żelazna Street, turning onto Leszno. She was too late! The youngsters had already come halfway across the ghetto in the sweltering heat, yet they marched along, by the barriers that blocked any escape, with confidence, in neat rows of four, dressed in their best clothes.

In that instant, Irena understood the doctor had not told them where they were going or why. She heard later that Dr. Korczak had refused to leave the children from the beginning, telling the German SS officer, "You do not leave a sick child in the night and you do not leave children at a time like this."

The officer had laughed. *Come then if you wish,* he told the doctor, and asked a twelve-year-old boy carrying a violin to play a tune.

The children had set off from the orphanage singing. Irena noticed the littlest ones clutched dolls in their hands. The dolls she had smuggled past the guards, the dolls Dr. Witwicki, her old university professor, had carved for them. She saw Dr. Korczak walking alongside the boys and girls, his face a mask of hard-fought self-control. She knew he'd become frail, and must be struggling like his charges, but his back was straight. In his arms, he carried one of the weary toddlers.

*Am I dreaming?* Irena thought. *How is this possible? These children are blameless. Walking to their deaths.*

As they passed, the doctor's eyes met Irena's. He did not

stop, nor greet her. He did not smile. He said nothing. Dr. Korczak kept walking.

Only a handful of pedestrians braved the street that day, and they scuttled with their heads down, anxious to be invisible to the SS soldiers who accompanied the children. At the *Umschlagplatz*, the guards drove the people selected for that day's deportations into the holding pen. Germans, Ukrainians, and Jewish policemen towered over the children's heads, barking orders and swinging their whips and rifle butts. After the chaos and bruising gauntlet, the children and the doctor waited in the loading area as the blazing sun crossed the sky.

The railway cars were loaded in the evening. Nachum and Ala saw the children at the last moment. Nachum rushed to the doctor's side. His characteristic calm deserted him. With wild eyes, he begged Dr. Korczak to come with him, to talk to the Germans. *We will ask the Judenräte for a postponement, Doctor. Please, come with me. We can stop this.* The old man shook his head. *I cannot leave the children even for a moment.*

The children, frightened, turned to Dr. Korczak for guidance, and the doctor looked sadly at Nachum for a long, last instant. Then turning his back on Nachum and the ghetto, he ushered the children into the windowless boxcar. Holding a tired child in each arm, the doctor stepped in behind them. Soldiers rolled the doors shut, pressing the many small bodies tight together, then wired the doors closed, and the train rattled down the tracks into the night.

Irena could not console herself. "I used my last ounce of strength to walk into the house," she said. "Then I had a nervous breakdown, and my mother had to call a doctor."

After Dr. Korczak and his orphans were deported, Irena wanted more than ever for her friends in the ghetto to leave and save themselves. One evening in the first week or two of August, Irena visited Ala in the dingy attic where she lived on Smocza Street. A window looked out over the rooftops of the ghetto. The two friends sat together, holding hands, watching the sun setting. Ala was sad and serious. Irena pleaded with her.

Rami, Ala's daughter, was safe on the Aryan side. Arek was with the partisans in forests outside Warsaw, part of a Jewish fighting group preparing for an armed resistance against the Germans. Ala was in constant communication with the underground; she had a pass and she could walk out of the ghetto if she wanted to.

Irena knew a safe place with friends where Ala could go into hiding. She would hide Ala at her own apartment if needed. She begged her friend. *Ala, in this envelope, there are identity papers. Take them.* Ala let them rest on the table between them.

*Irena, look at me.* Ala gestured to her face. Irena understood. She could not pretend that Ala's dark complexion, with sharp Jewish features were not "bad" looks. Papers would not save Ala if the Germans came looking. And, besides, she had her work here in the ghetto. For now, Ala let the papers lay untouched.

Some of their friends had already fled the ghetto, Adam, Jozef and his wife and son. Irena tried to persuade her. *There is no shame in living, Ala.* Ala's longtime collaborator, Dr. Hirszfeld, had escaped through the crypts that ran beneath the All Saints' Church, guided by Jan Zabinski, the zookeeper in Warsaw and an officer in the clandestine Home Army. Irena had been to the zoo to visit with the dozens of refugees hiding in the empty animal cages.

Ala did not fault the doctor. She was not a woman prepared to judge the actions of others when these were the stakes. There was no right or wrong, in Ala's mind; there were only the dictates of circumstance and conscience.

Through the hours of the evening, the two friends talked, Ala waging a quiet, but intense battle with herself. Her daughter was out beyond the walls, her husband in the forest, fighting, but the ghetto held her work, her responsibilities, the others whom she also loved: the sick, the old, the children. Irena understood because she, too, felt torn between wanting to save the children, and wanting to save herself. Finally, Irena went home.

### Ala Gołab-Grynberg

Ala sat awake for a long while considering. Irena's envelope still rested on the table at her elbow. Finally, she decided.

Picking up a stub of pencil and smoothing out a small piece of paper, Ala began to write what she knew might be a final letter, a good-bye to her young, beloved daughter. She addressed it to Jadwiga Strzawecka, the friend and orphanage director on the Aryan side who was caring for Rami. "I give my child in your care, raise my child as if it was yours," she wrote. And then, at last, she put her hand out to touch the identity papers. She already knew she would never use them. She tucked them firmly away in her satchel. In the morning, she would give them away to another Jewish woman on the street—the ultimate gift of survival.

Ewa Rechtman remained in the ghetto as well. Irena continued to bring food and medicine to her whenever possible. These days Ewa's usually well-made-up face was slipping. Wan and emaciated, her features remained recognizably Jewish. And, like Ala, Ewa also could not bring herself to leave her children at the youth circle. Not while every day the little ones were disappearing in the round-ups. Irena saw that for the abandoned youngsters, Ewa was "mother, father, sister, and friend. And they, in turn, became her biggest consolation."

Irena continued to hope her friends could escape the *Selektions* and survive the war, but in her heart she understood the need to continue to stand against the evil of the Nazis, even at the risk of one's life. After all, that was the

Ala's daughter, Rami Gołab-Grynberg, and Elżbieta Strzelecka, the daughter of the family who hid her. *Courtesy of the Gołab-Grynberg Family*

decision she made each morning, and she could not expect her friends to do any different.

One beautiful day in mid-August, Irena approached the ghetto checkpoint and presented her pass. She had come through so many times now in the last year that her heart didn't pound quite so much. But she always had to steel herself after being waved through by the guards, muster some defense against the smell of human waste, and now in the heat of the summer, the stench of decaying flesh. The bodies could not be collected as quickly as they fell. At any moment, there was some sound of human agony, a cry, a moan, a shriek, the hungry mewing of a child, and since the *Selektions* had started, the ever-present gunshots. All these assaults on her senses had become characteristic of life inside these walls.

And today Irena heard terrible news through the ghetto grapevine. Hordes of well-armed German troops had cordoned off the southernmost section of the walled district. All the streets beyond Plac Mirowski were sealed. Everyone inside forced to march to the deportation train platforms.

*Ewa!* Irena gasped. That was Ewa's neighborhood.

Ewa and her orphan children were trapped, and Irena would risk anything to save them. She had good connections in the ghetto medical corps and now commandeered an ambulance. They revved it up and took off. Careening south, her hands shaking, Irena decided they would use the same ruse that Ala seemed to be getting away with.

Somehow she had to convince the guards that Ewa was too weak to travel. Or they would hide her somewhere. They had done it enough times with the children. Irena reached the blocked streets and jumped out, her epidemic control badge in hand. She pulled up her most official voice. *I'm on urgent and authorized business. A medical mission.* If they could only get to Ewa The guards remained stoic and unconvinced. Irena drove to the next street, where her plea was again denied. Frantically, she drove the ambulance another route. When it was cut off, they tried another.

Finally, one young guard hesitated. Across the barrier Irena heard a harsh German voice yelling orders, dogs barked, gunshots . . . a scream of anguish. The guard's eyes hardened and he waved her away. At every turn, she was refused permission to enter the sealed neighborhood during the *Aktion*. Late that afternoon, Irena had to admit defeat. With an overwhelming grief and sense of hopelessness, she knew Ewa was lost among the heaving masses of bodies being shoved into the hot airless cattle cars. She'd seen how they crammed people in tightly and fastened the doors. Maybe Ewa had already breathed her last breath.

She tried to remember Ewa as she had been before the war, sitting with friends at a sidewalk table enjoying coffee, laughing and talking. Rachela was gone, too. Only she and Ala were left.

Irena had been suffering nightmares for some time. After the Nazis took Ewa, the horrible dreams grew worse. She always woke tired, feeling that at night in her sleep she relived the brutality she saw every day. Irena's dreams of Ewa repeated night after night, the same futile race to save her friend. The only mercy in her nighttime torments was the occasional whisper of Ewa's voice. Like always, it sounded "quiet, soothing, and full of kindness."

Not much later the Jewish policemen informed on Ala and Nachum, and Irena feared she would lose them, too. The police alerted the Nazis that their small medical station was in fact a smuggling base to spirit Jews away from the *Umschlagplatz*. Some policemen could be bribed to let doomed Jews slip through the searches. But the policemen didn't appreciate the doctors and nurses doing it for nothing. By informing on their fellow Jews, they could also gain favor with the Germans in hopes of saving themselves from deportation

One of the policemen, his conscience uneasy, broke rank and warned Ala and Nachum that they were being watched. The Germans had only to find them helping one person escape to execute them. The doctors and nurses did not return to their outpost. They had saved several hundred people, but Ala and Nachum's rescue mission had come to an end.

When the clinic folded, Ala kept one of the ambulances and turned again to helping Irena's network carry on smuggling children through the gates. Irena saw clearly that every child in the ghetto was destined for Treblinka. Irena knew "the only way to save the children was to get them out."

# 11

## *Time Running Out*

**"Volunteers" for Bread— August–September 1943**

By mid-August the Nazis had cleared much of the Warsaw ghetto. They worked in orderly sections and sent 190,000 people to their deaths at Treblinka. The open-air street markets had disappeared and only a trickle of food made it into the Jewish Quarter through underground channels. During the first three weeks of deportations, many of the remaining Jews had eaten little to nothing. Throngs of people went willingly to the loading platforms for one reason: the Germans had changed tactics and promised six pounds of bread and two pounds of jam to those who "volunteered" for relocation.

The smell of freshly baked bread but a few yards down the street proved irresistible. So what if death awaited them in the east, people reasoned? A certain death from starvation awaited them here.

At the *Umschlagplatz,* hundreds queued, waiting patiently for days, before getting a chance to get on the train. A witness reported, "The trains, already leaving twice a day with 12,000 people each, are unable to hold them all."

Once in a great while, on a train headed east to Treblinka, someone might get a chance to cheat death. Was it luck? The good fortune of better health and stronger muscles? Or a fierce will to live? Probably all these things had to fall your way, as they did for Regina Mikelberg, after she was loaded at the *Umschlagplatz* onto one of the death trains that summer. As the door sealed shut on the dozens trapped inside the fetid cattle cars, Regina grew frantic. When the cars rolled slowly away from Warsaw, the cries of fear and the rising stench were too much for the slender thirty-year-old woman. She had a sister still in the ghetto. She had her family. And she knew about Irena's network. She had been at the university with Janka Grabowska and Irena. If only she could get free, Janka would find somewhere to hide her. In the sweltering heat of the railway car, where body pushed against body, a dim ray of light shone through a small, dirty ventilation window. It was a narrow opening. Regina, though, was thin and determined. She pulled herself up toward the opening and a man below let her put a foot on his shoulder. His sad, knowing eyes urged her to risk it. With a mighty push, Regina threw herself through the window and onto

Jews marched to the *Umschlagplatz* for deportation at the end of the Jewish ghetto uprising, Spring 1943. *National Archives and Records Administration, College Park Instytut Pamieci Narodowej Panstwowe Muze*

the hard tracks below. Without looking back, she ran and ran into the darkness.

In the ghetto the roundups continued, and the Jews who remained behind went into hiding in their attics and basements. Even those with work papers or Judenräte protection knew better than to risk being seen when a neighborhood was emptied. But, to the world beyond the walls, the Nazi extermination of the Jewish population remained largely and conveniently invisible. Jews in Warsaw and the people in Poland helping them knew that their only hope would come from abroad. Would the British and the Americans send help in time?

## The Question of Baptism

As August passed, too quickly turning to September, Irena and her friends worked at a ferocious pace. She had no qualms knocking on doors and begging Jewish families to trust her with the lives of their children.

Ushered into their cramped apartments, Irena made her plea to families in despair. Disagreement over sending the children away often splintered relationships. Fathers would say yes. Grandparents would say no. Mothers wept inconsolably. The choices were appalling. Irena could not guarantee safety, and furthermore, most of the Jewish children were hidden from the Nazis by taking on Catholic identities. It was the easiest way to protect them, especially the babies. With baptism came a new set of authentic church records and documents that did not have to be faked or manufactured.

Many parents threw aside questions of religion. *Save my child,* they told Irena. *Do what you must to save my daughter.* But when Irena explained what might have to happen, some Jewish parents shook their heads and refused to give her their children. "Jewish religious law is clear," some Orthodox fathers told her. "We cannot exile our children from the Jewish nation simply to save them now." Sometimes she would try again the following day and find everyone in the building had been taken to the *Umschlagplatz.*

Irena knew that Jewish families across the ghetto debated this and called upon the rabbis to guide them. The Nazi plan for Polish Jews could not be denied, and she understood the rabbi's quandary. "If more than 300,000 Jews are to be annihilated in Warsaw, what is the use of saving several hundred children? Let them perish or survive together with the entire community."

Irena saw the agony of parents compelled to agree to the erasure of their children's identity. The scenes replayed themselves in Irena's nightmares. She made her peace with a solemn promise to the parents—despite the dangers it created, she kept a list of the children's real names and families, a list that continued to grow longer.

The day came when Irena had to tell Bieta Koppel's family the infant would be baptized. She knew the baby's father, Josel, was gone. He had been shot on the platform

Jewish child in hiding poses outside in a garden wearing her First
Communion dress, 1943. *United States Holocaust Memorial Museum, courtesy
of Alicia Fajnsztejn Weinsberg*

of the *Umschlagplatz*, when he refused to board the cattle cars to Treblinka. But Bieta's mother, Henia, and grandfather, Aron Rochman, were still alive in the ghetto at the end of the summer.

Bieta had stayed hidden at the home of Stanislawa Bussold, who'd made up some story to explain to nosy neighbors how a woman in her late fifties happened to suddenly have at home a crying six-month-old. Soon, in the normal course of things, Bieta would move on to permanent shelter. When she did, no one but Irena would know where Bieta was going and that Henia and Josel Koppel were her parents. It was a chain of knowing as fragile as Irena's life and a flimsy bit of paper, but it was for Bieta's safety.

Irena continued keeping lists of the children's real names and their new identities as well as their current addresses. If the lists fell into the wrong hands, well, that didn't bear thinking about. This information had to be kept for the children's families to find them after the war. The space on that scrap of paper, next to the entry "Elżbieta Koppel," where the baby's new Polish name would go, had remained empty.

Back in the ghetto, still working in Toebbens's factory, Henia ached for her daughter. A few times she found a telephone in the ghetto and called Stanislawa's apartment. Henia asked nothing in those moments except that Stanislawa hold the telephone close, so she could listen for a few moments to Bieta coo and babble. On the distant end of the line Henia wept quietly. Though Henia knew the wild risk to herself, her baby, and Stanislawa, once or twice she could not help herself. She slipped out of the ghetto for a few hours to hold her baby.

In early autumn, Irena learned a Catholic identity had been found or forged for Bieta and she would be baptized. On the scrap of paper, next to the entry "Elżbieta Koppel," would be penciled "Stefcia Rumkowski." Irena knew that cutting off Bieta from her Jewish faith and ethnicity would make the loss of the baby even more painful for Henia and Aron. But she could not keep this news from them. It was important for her to be honest with these families who were losing everything.

On a crisp morning, Irena stood outside the checkpoint where the slave labor gangs left the ghetto on their way to work in German factories. Bieta's grandfather sometimes joined this sad column of men, who labored long days for small bits of food. Yes. There was Aron, eyes down, marching briskly at the shouted commands of the guards. Irena walked along, pretending no interest in the workers. The Nazis did not allow Poles and Jews to speak to each other.

She caught Aron's eye and in a quick rush of words she told him Bieta would be baptized. *I had to tell you.* Aron looked away. There on the street, amidst the footsteps of strangers and the ruin of war, Irena watched, thinking her own heart would break, as the older man broke down and cried for the loss of his granddaughter. She longed to reach out for Aron's hand, but she did not. She did not want to endanger him any more than she had. She turned and walked away with heavy steps.

A few days later, Stanislawa told Irena a package had come for Bieta. Inside lay an exquisite lace christening gown and a bright gold crucifix for the baby, wrapped carefully in tissue paper. There was no note. There was no need for one. This gift, so costly in heart, as well as zloty, was a family's good-bye to its precious baby, and an expression of hope that beyond the terrors of the ghetto, lay a future.

## Ala Gołab-Grynberg

By early September, Ala was heartsick beyond what she had thought a human could bear. The ghetto was nearly empty. She believed the Nazis planned to kill the entire Jewish population of Poland. Knowing that Rami was safe on the Aryan side was her consolation. She continued her nursing at the hospital on Leszno Street. And when ambulances trundled across the checkpoints, filled with supplies and linens, Ala packed in stowaway children as well. Sometimes those children were sent on to Irena and Jan Dobraczyński. But Ala had contacts in the underground with other people running other rescue operations.

On September 6, at the Leszno medical clinic, the skeleton staff called an urgent meeting. Ala was tired. She leaned against the wall and listened. The doctor's voice rose with panic as he explained the latest German orders.

Everyone in the ghetto, even the patients in their crowded wards, must report that day for a final registration at the *Umschlagplatz*.

Ala gasped. The sick and bedridden patients could not march to the railway platforms. Neither could the elderly and children. Doctors and nurses had tried to save their own elderly parents and small children by registering them as patients. Patients they would now have to help deport. The realization dawned on one nurse's face, and she broke down crying. Once again, Ala scoured her brain for ways to keep these innocent people out of the Nazi's murderous hands. Before she could do anything, the SS and police stormed the building, ready to liquidate the hospital population. Ala stood frozen. She turned to a young nurse with big, fearful eyes, and she could not reassure her. *Oh, God . . .* It would be Dr. Korczak's walk to the *Umschlagplatz* all over again.

Gunmen stomped through the wards. Going bed to bed they executed the delirious and immobile. They lined up patients who could walk. They'd walk in their flimsy hospital gowns to the *Umschlagplatz*, or as far as they could make it. Nurses and doctors rushed into rooms ahead of police, desperate to save their own children and parents from this final terror. Hands shaking, they poured precious doses of cyanide into the mouths of sons and daughters. They would die in Treblinka, or on the way. Cyanide allowed them to die quietly. One doctor, weeping, turned to a nurse and asked her to administer the fatal dose to his father.

But Ala wasn't ready to give up yet. Racing to the children's ward, she whispered to a duty nurse, *Run, tell the kitchen we are coming.* She needed them to fill a truck with food and empty vegetable boxes. *Tell them to hurry!*

She clapped her hands. *Children! We must line up now, quickly.* Ala maintained her best calm face, urging the children to move fast without scaring them. Nurses carried two or three infants at a time. Daisy chains of toddlers and bossy four-year-olds held each other's hands and followed Ala down the back staircase and into the kitchens. They loaded thirty children in and among the wooden potato boxes. The cook jumped in the cab of the truck and drove, disappearing around the street corner. Hundreds of little tykes in the hospital could not be saved, but for now, Ala chose to think about the ones who got away.

With the hospital empty, Ala joined the ranks of Jews working for the Germans. Those with strong constitutions, capable of surviving hours of grueling labor, had a chance at life by working in German workshops, work gangs, and factories. Ala joined baby Bieta's mother, Henia Koppel, and Nachum Remba in Walter Toebbens's factory.

Of the 450,000 people sent to the ghetto, Ala heard a rumor that the Nazis planned to keep some 30,000 Jews for slave labor. Another some 30,000 residents, including those in the Jewish resistance, and many with children, had burrowed into cellars, attics, burnt-out buildings, and even dug secret tunnels in hopes of surviving. The deportations paused in mid-September, but everyone knew the soldiers wouldn't stop until they had rooted out the Jews burrowed in the ghetto. The hunt for Jews who had fled to the Aryan side geared up. Posters tacked across the city offered amnesty to people who turned in Jews they were shielding.

# 12

## Crisis

As Irena and her network raced the timetable of rail cars rumbling east from the *Umschlagplatz*, crisis struck. There were many expenses to hiding people: food, rent, medical supplies, even bribes to be paid. Irena knew that soon, no matter how brave any of them were, saving more children would be impossible because money was running out.

The families and institutions protecting the children needed financial support for the basic costs of food and clothing. Wealthy ghetto parents had paid for the support of their children in advance and trusted Irena with the money. She felt morally obligated to account for that money and make sure it was spent according to the parents' wishes.

People on the Aryan side of Warsaw were allotted a ration of 699 calories per day, a starvation diet. Irena hated to ask people to take in the children of strangers without offering them money to buy additional food for their family on the black market. Two or three extra kilograms of black-market butter, or double that amount of sugar, cost nearly five hundred zlotys. The cost of those goods had increased fifteen-fold under German occupation, but the workers' wages had not kept up.

For some families, a couple pounds of butter would cost an entire month's salary. Despite the financial hardship, half of Irena's foster families refused to take money from her. Others could not survive without payment. The last inhabitants of the ghetto were financially ruined, and Irena and her friends did not have vast incomes. When Irena looked at the account books, she could see everything they had worked so hard to accomplish unraveling.

One day in early December, Irena sat in her office stewing. Her old metal desk was scattered with notes and bits of paper, and there was hardly room to move her chair around in the small office, where she spent her days jammed in among the file cabinets. In the corridor of the welfare office, the *tap-tap-tap* of someone's sturdy heels came and went, and Irena thought that whoever it was hesitated outside her doorway for a moment. Irena realized she was biting on her pencil. She was stressed. It was worse than that, Irena told herself sharply. Stress didn't even begin to cover it. The wind battered the window glass, and Irena pulled her sweater closer around her. She was facing disaster.

She had her lists—those bits of tissue-thin paper with

the names and addresses of hundreds of hidden children—safely hidden. She would never work on those in the office. But she couldn't help trying to work out some troubling sums on a piece of scrap paper. When Irena looked at the figures she had scratched out, there was no way to make it all add up.

She spent her waking hours preoccupied with finding money to keep her hidden children alive. She'd begun this venture by diverting welfare supplies and money in the city offices. Even now, if she could fiddle the paperwork, municipal resources could continue to pay for the needs of the Jewish children. But that was becoming harder and harder as the city coffers dwindled.

Irena knew that the Germans had become suspicious of her and they were watching. They had found irregularities in the social welfare offices and clamped down on funding. So far, they had not discovered Irena's and Irka's falsified records, but for some other misdemeanor, real or imagined, the director of their division of welfare services had been shipped to another German death camp, named Auschwitz.

As Irena deliberated, a shadow fell over her and she shivered. She looked up to see her colleague Stefania Wichlińska at the office door. *Do you have a moment?* Irena slid her scrap of figures into a budget file, then threw up her hands in mock despair at the many files on her desk. Stefania smiled and dropped into the rickety little chair across from her. After a few minutes of small talk, Stefania bent and spoke hushed, quick words in Irena's ear. Irena kept her face blank. Stefania stood to leave, but waited, holding Irena's gaze. A long moment passed before Irena nodded. Stefania walked away and Irena went back to the files in front of her.

She couldn't remember what she'd been doing, and the only thing on her mind now was a question. A huge question. Should she follow Stafania's instructions? Could whispered words be a trap? The Nazis had ways of turning people against one another. Under sufficient pressure, friends and neighbors went along with Gestapo fishing schemes, helping the enemy catch people harboring Jews.

Stefania had given Irena very little information and no way to verify the source of the instructions. In this warped world of Nazi occupation, with Warsaw's people ripped apart by brutality and deprivation, both friend and foe would communicate like this. A short cryptic message. Should Irena trust Stefania? That was the question. And she had little time to decide the answer.

## Code Name Żegota

Dark comes early in Warsaw winters, and it was falling when Irena walked toward Żurawia Street a day or two after Stefania had whispered the address in her ear. She'd decided to trust her coworker and follow the directions. She would not second-guess herself now, when she was approaching number 24 Żurawia Street. She let herself in the apartment building and walked up to the third floor, number 4.

Irena rapped a quick knock on the door. A woman's voice asked, *Who's there?*

*Trojan,* said Irena.

That was the password she'd been given. The door opened. Irena stepped into the dim apartment. All the shades were drawn tightly over the windows. The gray-haired woman who let her in appeared nervous, her face flushed. There was a man, too. He beckoned Irena, and she followed the two through a series of doorways to a small room at the back of the apartment.

There Irena met a second man, who was introduced as Trojan. She was introduced as Jolanta. Irena kept her face stony as she faced him, determined to reveal nothing. But her mind was racing. Trojan was a stocky man, with a thick neck and a dark beard, and his eyes gleamed with intelligence under a pair of wild and bushy black eyebrows. The moment of truth had come. If these people were informers, she'd incriminated herself just by coming here. A terrible gamble.

Irena remained silent. Trojan spoke. In low tones he described a secret network, code name: Żegota. It had been called the Council for Jewish Relief until the group decided the word "Jewish" was too dangerous. Żegota had been founded by two women, a far-right Catholic nationalist like Jan Dobraczyński, and a left-leaning Catholic Socialist more like Irena. From opposite sides of the political spectrum, they came together in condemning the genocide of the Jews, and trying to do something concrete to help their Jewish countryman. Żegota had connections with the Polish underground. Were Ala and Nachum also working with this group? There was something familiar here.

*Would Irena and her network join Żegota?* Trojan's question hung in the silence.

Seeing her hesitation, the man jumped in to say no one in Żegota would interfere in Irena's current operations. She liked the sound of that. Her greatest concern was the safety of her operatives and the hundreds of children in hiding. Then Trojan mentioned money, and Irena sat up and listened. He explained that Żegota's funds came from agents in London, dropped into Poland by parachute. To heck with the risks—she needed money.

*Yes.* Irena looked him squarely in the eye and stuck her hand out to shake on it.

Trojan laughed. "Well, Jolanta, we're striking a good deal together. You have a team of trusted people, and we have the necessary funds to help a larger number of people."

With Żegota's funds Irena immediately started paying monthly stipends to foster families, and she made plans to expand operations. Her friend Adam had escaped the ghetto, but had grown restless with being cooped up in hiding. Irena put him in charge of managing money for her network and keeping track of the growing volume of identity papers. Not her secret lists of the Jewish children's real names, but the paperwork for their new identities.

This allowed Irena to focus her efforts on the practical aspects of caring for the hidden children. Irena went from leading a network of old college friends, prewar political comrades, and coworkers, to heading a large web connected with the Polish underground.

Jaga, Irka, Ala, and Jadwiga remained the base of her network, but it had expanded with the help of dozens more couriers and operatives. Maria and Henryk Palester, the couple who had refused to move into the ghetto, offered their apartment as a standby point in Irena's network. The apartment also sheltered Maria Proner and her twelve-year-old daughter Janina. Janina was best friends from school with Maria and Henryk's daughter Malgorzata.

The Polish nurse Helena Szeszko organized a number of doctors, including Dr. Majkowski, who had given Irena her ghetto pass, into a system of medical hideouts. This allowed for Jewish children and adults to get long or short term medical care without risking a trip out in the open where they might be recognized. Most of Irena's cohorts knew nothing about Żegota because she was the only point of contact.

Jan Dobraczyński's signature allowed hundreds of Jewish children into Catholic orphanages. Jaga Piotrowska arranged these transports, often to rural areas hundreds of miles away. More than two hundred children would go to the Father Boduen Home, where Wladyslawa Marynowska and Irka Schultz were now the primary operatives. Jadwiga Deneka crisscrossed Warsaw and much of central Poland, checking on the youngsters' welfare and delivering the financial support. Many families opened their homes as emergency shelters for the Jewish children, taking an immense risk with the safety of their own children and family members. Irena's apartment became a last-resort emergency safe house.

Irena's budget added up to a fortune each month; some months she handled some 250,000 zlotys (about three-quarters of a million of today's dollars). The money came from sources in the Polish government in exile in Britain and from the Jewish-American community. Conscious of the sacred trust placed in them, she and Adam kept careful records of every zloty. The money enabled them, by January of 1943, to count more than a thousand names on the growing list of rescued children. They'd truly been snatched from the rail cars of death, and every single child Irena had hidden was still alive, a winning streak that could easily end any day.

## Jaga Piotrowska

Jaga had worked alongside Irena and Jadwiga since the first meeting at Irena's house three years ago. They had seen nights of frantic action rendezvousing with fresh escapees and guiding them to Irena's emergency rooms, or safe houses for the children in their first hours outside the ghetto. Jaga had turned her own house on Lekarska Street into one of these, though she lived on a busy street near a hospital for German soldiers. People came and went from her house at all hours without raising suspicion because there was a door at the back and front. But the operation was at greatest risk when Jaga transported a child through the streets in daylight, which she sometimes had to do.

Jaga paid close attention to every movement when she was out and about on the Aryan side with younger children. Handling the three- or four-year-olds sometimes felt like handling explosives. Too young to censor themselves, in a single moment they could blow their cover—which is exactly what happened one day on her way to deliver a youngster to a safe hose. They had boarded one of Warsaw's trams, which were small boxy cars that rattled along tracks across the city. The boy, small and skinny, was nervous, his eyes darting around. As the tram clanked to one stop and the next, he grew more skittish.

Jaga worried as the tram filled with passengers and more than a dozen people crammed into the small boxcar. She and the boy sat at the front of the car and Jaga hoped the view would distract him. When he started to cry, Jaga talked to him in a low soothing voice, but he only sobbed louder and then with no warning, began calling for his mother. In Yiddish.

One by one, conversations died until the tram fell silent. Jaga registered the startled looks in her direction, the dawning horror of those jammed in the streetcar with her. *Yiddish. That child is Jewish.* Jaga dared not look around, as she sensed the growing fury of the woman next to her. Should the Germans happen along, everyone on the tram would be complicit. Jaga could see the tram driver understood this, too.

With a rush of fear, Jaga's world narrowed to one thought. At the next stop, would someone betray them to the police? It was too likely. A vein of anti-Semitic feeling ran through many of the Polish citizens of Warsaw, and blackmailers abounded, waiting for just this type of opportunity.

Jaga tensed. Her panic rose. She reminded herself that she had to be brave for the child's sake. She leaned near the tram driver. *Please, help me,* she whispered.

He did not take his eyes from the track stretching in front of him. Jaga felt the weight of what would come. She and the boy might be shot right there on the tram. She thought of her daughter, not much older than this boy. A moment later the tram jolted. Everyone inside the vehicle lurched through several more jolts before the car screeched to a stop. Shopping bags tipped. A piece of bruised fruit rolled under the benches. A man swore quietly and turned to help an older lady right herself. Jaga calculated her chances of fleeing with the child. She would not get far.

While the passengers gathered their wits, the tram driver bellowed, "Okay, everyone out! The tram is broken, I'm returning to the depot."

He opened the doors and waved the passengers out. Jaga lifted the child to her hip, preparing to step down into the street and take their chances. The odds were against them. The driver shook his head. *Not you. You stay.* He gestured for her to get down, and she obeyed. He put the empty train into gear and they rolled forward along the tracks, not stopping until they reached a quiet neighborhood with modest houses and small gardens. The driver slowed the tram to a stop. "You'll have to get off here," he said. "Good luck."

Jaga slumped for a moment as her tension slipped away. "Thank you." He shook his head and gave her a sad smile as she and the boy descended from the tram. Jaga never saw the driver again, nor learned his name.

## Teens in the Resistance

Many teenagers in occupied Poland risked their lives, too, stepping up for responsibilities well beyond their years. Both boys and girls joined the armed resistance in the ghetto and in the Home Army. Orphanages couldn't take in Jewish teenagers, and in foster homes, teens stood out more than younger children, raising dangerous questions. They lived on the streets, worked on farms in the country, or stayed completely out of sight like Jewish adults

Krzystof Palester (right), the teenaged son of Irena's friends Maria and Henryk Palester, with two female medics during the Warsaw Uprising.
*Photograph by Joachim Joachimczyk [public domain image]*

running from the Nazis. Many holed up in the ghetto, willing to fight to the death if it came to that. A number of Jewish teenagers joined Irena's network as couriers.

After the deportations ended in mid-September, guards controlled the checkpoints with alacrity. The Nazis discovered the courthouse escape route on Leszno Street, halting the flow of contraband there, both food and people. The options for escaping from the ghetto narrowed to a dangerous trip through miles of city sewer. Irena's teenage couriers guided families out through the underground pipes, and they carried in messages and money.

That winter the Polish resistance gathered strength across Warsaw and the Polish countryside. Many young people joined the guerrilla bands bent on harassing and sabotaging German forces. The Palesters' teenage son Krystof joined an elite squad of young people, whose missions included assassinations. The courts of the Polish underground tried and sentenced local Nazi functionaries and Gestapo collaborators. Every day brought news of three or four people executed by the resistance, and some of the most fearsome assassins were young women.

### Jerzy

Irena's collaborators found a safe house for two teenage boys, now going by the names Jurek and Jerzy, in Otwock—the village of her childhood. One day they narrowly escaped a Nazi roundup in the building where they had been staying, and now they were homeless. Hanging out in one of the city's downtown squares, they saw two teenage girls. Jurek stared at the pretty one with soft brown hair, hoping to catch her eye. When he did, their connection felt electric. They started talking and soon they were flirting. The girl's name was Anna, and when it came time for her to head home, not wanting to end the good time, she invited Jurek and Jerzy to come along.

When Anna came bouncing into the apartment with the two young strangers, her mother's face showed raw horror. Maria Kukulska turned and disappeared into the back bedroom. The teenagers heard murmurs of conversation and then a heated argument carried on in hushed voices.

Adam Celnikier, Irena's Jewish friend handling the accounting of Żegota funds, had been concealed at the Kukulska's apartment, and at this time the family was also shielding another Jewish man. Long minutes of awkward small talk passed before the bedroom door opened. A tiny blond woman with blazing blue eyes stepped out and greeted the boys. Anna's mother marched her into the bedroom, and Jurek could hear that she was in deep trouble. Her mother sounded furious. Then the small woman commanded his attention. Who were they, and what were they up to?

An old man in the ghetto had told Jurek the way to survive on the Aryan side was to forget who he had been.

Forget everything Jewish and act as if he were unconcerned. He mustered a brazen acting ability and hinted he and Jerzy were resistance fighters. The boys told the woman they had just narrowly escaped a Gestapo roundup of a safe house on Idzikowskiego Street. That much was true; they had survived by crawling out a rooftop window.

Perhaps the woman believed their story. Maybe it was obvious they were Jewish boys on the run from the ghetto. She listened to them, and then she nodded. That's all it took. The boys were allowed to stay, and introduced to Adam and the other Jewish man. Soon they were like part of the family. The woman was Irena.

# 13

## Toward the Precipice

Working with Żegota and her increased resources, Irena could help adults, as well as children, who needed to escape the Germans. She rented two rambling old buildings where she set up fake tuberculosis "rest clinics" to provide cover for Jewish adults and leaders of the resistance. These vulnerable adults became "new patients." Irena located one clinic, a center for tuberculosis treatment, in Otwock, where she had lived as a child with her papa and her mother, and the other in the nearby village of Swider.

In Swider, Mrs. Zusman, an elderly Jewish woman with "Aryan" looks and good identity papers, ran the day-to-day operations. A train line connected downtown Warsaw with the village, and the station at Swider was nothing more than a platform in the woods, making it easy for Irena to visit the modest villa often. Under the guise of a city social worker, she brought money, doctors, or forged identity papers. Irena stepped off the train one afternoon in January 1943, and set off by foot over the frozen ground to check in on five Jewish men staying at the villa. When she arrived, "Auntie" Zusman quickly welcomed her into the kitchen by the fire, and over a cup of tea the women settled down to business.

A short time later, a violent pounding came on the door. Judging by the noise, these visitors had not come for tea. Shouts ordered them to open the door and threatened to denounce them all to the Gestapo. Any hint they received of hidden Jews, the Gestapo investigated with gusto. Even if none were found, they often hauled off everyone in the house to Szucha Avenue for questioning. But giving in to blackmailers was a poor alternative. Blackmailers could bleed a family's resources and betray them to the Gestapo when the money dried up.

At the sound of the knocking, everyone jumped to their feet, and Irena grabbed the fake identity papers, which would be their death. She sent Mrs. Zusman a horrified look. The older woman shooed her and the others toward the back door.

*Coming, dearies, coming,* she called, clomping to the door and pretending to fiddle with the lock. She gained time for Irena and the others to slip out.

They scattered in all directions, the men heading far into the woods. Irena stopped in a quiet copse, her heart pounding. She feared for Mrs. Zusman's life, but she could not leave without knowing for sure. She hid the papers under a fallen stump and crept back toward the house.

The scene unfolding on the front doorstep astonished her.

Mrs. Zusman had not been arrested. Fearlessly, she was facing down the thugs, not Gestapo, but Polish blackmailers, *szmalcowniks*. Planting her hands on her hips, the older woman yelled at them, her eyes blazing. *How dare you foul bandits attack the peace of a Polish Christian!* She shouted with indignation. *I will have the Germans arrest you for abusing an old lady!*

Shocked, the blackmailers hesitated a moment on the doorstep. Rattled by Mrs. Zusman's shrill voice continuing to berate them, the blackmailers turned and ran. Irena and Mrs. Zusman had a good laugh, but now this safe house was "burned," as they called a place that was no longer safe. At a moment's notice, the Jews had to flee and Irena had to find them a new hiding place. Sometimes Irena had a place people on the run could take refuge, but many adult Jews moved house to house, cellar to attic, closet to hidey-hole in constant fear of capture.

Irena operated eight or nine different safe houses across the city to aid Jewish families who broke out of the ghetto. The Gestapo had uncovered information about her network's activity. They were now tracking a woman named Jolanta, but their clues had not led them to Irena yet.

She watched over her shoulder everywhere she went, in

fear of leading the Gestapo to her friends and to the children. Maria Kukulska's apartment became a meeting place for the Żegota cell, and Maria and Irena devised a way to communicate with codes and signals. On her approach to the Praga district, Irena scanned the faces of loitering strangers and eyed reflections in shop windows, trying to make sure she was not followed. In the same neighborhood, the underground was forging fake German stamps and identity papers in the old state mint on Markowska Street.

German soldiers came and went from their nearby barracks, and the Warsaw zoo was only a few blocks north. The zookeeper, Dr. Jan Zabinski, and his wife, Antonia, worked in the resistance, and Irena stopped at their white stucco bungalow on both business and pleasure, meeting Jewish friends or Żegota contacts.

Sometimes when Irena approached a rendezvous with a contact, she was gripped with fear. She changed her destination at the last minute and ducked into a shop or a laundry. On days when Irena felt certain nobody was tailing her, she looked for a sign in Maria's front window. The all clear signal told her the Gestapo or blackmailers hadn't been nosing about, and the hallways were clear of curious neighbors.

## A Nighttime Visit

A *tap-tap-tap* startled Irena from sleep. She squinted in the dark to make out the hands of the clock. Three in the morning. Her heart raced. She didn't let herself think about unannounced visitors, the Nazis coming for her in the middle of the night. They would come, eventually. But there was no sense in imagining it before it happened.

She heard the quiet rapping again, and reminded herself the Nazis would come with pounding boots, shouts, and the splintering of wood, aiming to terrorize the neighbors as well as to arrest the suspects. This light *tap-tap-tap* was the predawn signal of a conspirator.

Something must have gone sideways on tonight's rescue mission. Irena moved like a thief to the kitchen where her list of names rested on the table, under the window, as always. Just as she had practiced, Irena swept it all out the window. She leaned to watch the cigarette papers flutter to the ground and settle among the garbage cans. No one would notice a scrap with a few light pencil markings.

Irena glanced around the room to make sure all was in order and was grateful to hear the even wisps of her mother's breathing from the bedroom. She had not revealed any part of her clandestine activities to her mother, hoping to protect her when the worst came. Irena tied on her robe and went to the door. Sliding back the bolt, she opened it a crack to peer out.

At first she saw nothing but a glimpse of the door across the hall closing. Her neighbor had beaten her to the knock. In the stripe of soft moonlight thrown through the kitchen window into the hall, a teenager stood with four small children, all of them drenched in sewage.

"*Jolanta,*" the teenager whispered.

Irena didn't know the real name of this steely-eyed girl with a tangle of dark curls tucked under her cap. All the couriers in her network had code names like she did, though the true identity of Jolanta had become an open secret in the resistance. Under torture, a person could not say what they did not know, and so it was better not to ask the teenagers any questions. She beckoned the soggy group into her kitchen.

The teenager gave a small shrug. *I didn't know where else to go.* Irena nodded. She understood. That night, the network had planned to whisk a group of Jewish children through a secret passageway in the city's underground sewers. A guide was supposed to deliver them to one of the guardians.

The Nazis had run a patrol, the older girl told her. Some of the children had gotten lost. This was the stuff of Irena's nightmares. The soldiers had captured the sewer guide and other couriers. Likely, they would suffer brutal interrogations. The safe houses were compromised. Who knew what people might tell under torture, and there was no point in blaming anyone who cracked. Everyone in Warsaw knew—the Gestapo did unspeakable things to people.

Irena recognized the sad, frightened eyes of ghetto children on these shivering bundles of wet filth, and her chest tightened. They'd dressed them carefully, in their best and warmest clothing, a parent's last loving gesture. Her mind swung into action. She had other safe houses. If she needed, she could take the children to Jaga for the time being. But first they needed a good scrubbing and their clothes washed and dried, so she could sneak them back out of the apartment building before morning brought out nosy neighbors.

It was also the day one of her mother's friends came to visit, always at seven o'clock. Irena trusted her mother's friend—the Nazis had killed her husband—but not enough to share a secret like this. With the children's lives, she took no more risks than she had to.

They'd have until dawn, less time if her neighbor betrayed them. Irena had no idea what her neighbor believed about the Jews, and she did not want to find out now. The Gestapo might already be coming for them. If she were caught helping these children, death was certain for all of them, including her mother. But the children could not travel covered in the telltale muck of the sewer, nor could they risk breaking the nighttime curfew.

Irena took her largest pot and began heating water. Hot water and plenty of soap were her best weapons to fight the grunge, and typhoid. The sewage was swimming with the disease that had killed her father. As the girl and the children began undressing, Irena rinsed their clothes in the sink with a tiny sliver of precious soap, and then scrubbed her hands well and beneath her nails. Soon the little trousers and shifts were rung out and left to dry near the heater. They would still be damp come morning, but this was the best she could do.

She hurried the children to the bath, warning them to tiptoe. Footsteps at this hour would make the downstairs neighbors suspicious. When she saw her mother standing in the doorway watching her, unsteady on her legs due to her chronic illness, Irena's heart sank. The four little naked children and the dark-haired teenager needed no explanation. There was only acceptance and worry in her mother's eyes, but Irena hated to endanger her like this.

The children climbed into the tub, relaxing their guard a bit in the warm water. After washing the first three, Irena warmed the water for the last child. Reaching for a new bar of soap, she realized there was no more. Before the war, there had always been plenty of soap made from animal fats and ashes. But this winter, lard and bacon drippings were gourmet meals. Better to be dirty than hungry. Irena and her mother could afford only small amounts of lye soap to do their laundry.

*Soap?* Her mother shook her head. There was nothing left but the small half sliver in the kitchen, now a thin and flabby wafer, not enough to wash the oldest child. Irena sighed. A bar of soap might cost them everything.

She thought for a long moment, weighing the risks,

before slipping out of the apartment. The neighbor had already seen the children; if she hadn't reported them yet, maybe she wouldn't. Irena drew a breath and knocked quietly.

Only an instant passed before the door opened a smidgen. *Soap?* Irena whispered. *I can't sleep. I am doing my laundry.* It was four a.m. but the old woman wasn't sleeping either. She turned without a word, leaving the door cracked. Irena waited. The skin on the back of her neck prickled. Had the woman gone to call the Gestapo?

The harsh light in the hallway showed the nicks and scratches in the woodwork and where years of footsteps had worn the treads on the stairs. Irena's muscles tensed, ready to run, but she ignored her body's danger signals. There was nowhere to run to. And she could never desert the children. She must brave this out. The sound of soft footsteps came from behind the door, and a wrinkled hand thrust something toward her, something wrapped in a bit of moist paper. Irena took the offering from the warm, soft hand. *Thank you,* she whispered. *You are welcome,* came the hushed reply.

Just as dawn began to light the streets of Warsaw that cool morning, Irena sent her charges on their way. The teenage girl walked out the front door of the building, hand-in-hand with four well-turned-out if slightly damp small children. The morning breeze blew at their coats, and the children set a brisk pace, the girl with the cap pulling them closer. A few moments more and they turned the corner, lost from Irena's view.

## More Close Calls

The urgent call for help sometimes came right from the top of Żegota. Trojan himself would send word: Irena was needed in the forest outside Otwock, where a woman was hiding in a garbage bin with her infant daughter. The baby was dying. *Would Irena bring a doctor she trusted?* And Irena did.

Another day Trojan sent an urgent message for Irena to meet him at the train station. In the dingy building, she scanned the crowds, looking for Trojan. Over the loudspeaker, she heard a muffled voice read out track numbers and departure times, and behind her the roar of trains arriving and leaving. At the last minute, she saw him, but barely recognized him. His tuberculosis had worsened, aging him years since she'd last seen him. Irena greeted him with a warm smile, then waited as he coughed into his bloodstained handkerchief, and they boarded just as the doors closed. When the train pulled away and picked up speed toward the rural Wawer district, Trojan explained their mission. *I have a name,* he said, handing her a scrap of paper. *Somewhere in the village they are concealing a Jewish child who survived a massacre. She saw the soldiers kill her mother. They say she is hysterical.* Irena understood they would need to proceed with the utmost caution. One could never predict the behavior of a traumatized child.

But trouble came sooner than expected. As they changed trains for their first connection, Irena turned to lift down her bag filled with supplies. She tried to be prepared for whatever a child might need. Suddenly, a man shouted gruff orders in German, the crowd surge forward, a man cried out in pain. Irena glanced at her bag. Trojan hissed. *Roundup! Leave it.* The two slipped off the platform and scrambled between two carriages to the other side of the tracks. Trojan stopped, leaning against the carriage, trying to muffle his coughing. This was too much for an old man with tuberculosis. Irena couldn't let him go on. The voices of the soldiers moved closer, and they crouched low beside the carriage. Did Trojan have the strength to run? *Please, let me go alone. I can get the child. You should return to the city.*

*What?* He flashed her a grin. *You have me for a loser who cannot escape the Germans?* Irena did not have to admit her worries because at that moment the carriage behind them started moving. The train pulled away, in the direction of Wawer at last, and Trojan swung himself up and stuck out his hand to grasp Irena's.

They arrived in the village in good time, and set out to look for the girl. Without an address, it was no easy task to find a small child in the village, a child people were hiding in fear for her life, and theirs. A wrong question here, a suspect word there, and the mission would fail. They looked for the girl late into the night, and when they found her at last, Trojan pulled up a chair beside the weeping child and tenderly stroked her hair in a silence that seemed to go on forever. At last, the tearstained face opened to him, and the girl pulled herself onto his lap and clung tight. *"I don't want to be here,"* she whispered into his shoulder. *"Take me with you."*

Trojan and Irena shared a glance. He squeezed the child tighter, and she smiled, glad in this moment to see his eyes watering, too.

With so many children passing through their hands, Irena and her team remembered them best by small, heart-breaking details: the baby in the garbage can, the girl with a red bow, or the boy with the green jacket. Other times, they were the children of friends; many of the rescued had some connection to someone in the group—friends of friends, the neighbors of families, old acquaintances . . . all part of a web of trust.

The safety of the web and everyone it connected depended upon the strength of each individual. And on luck.

### Jaga Piotrowska

Jaga had dozens of Jewish people staying at her house at some time or another. It was an emergency stop for people in trouble. One beautiful morning in May, Jaga found her-self in a dire situation. The Germans started a search of all the houses on Lekarska Street. Several Jewish children and adults were staying in Jaga's house.

Her house had special advantages. That was why so many people came and went from Jaga's. Jaga was forty years old in 1943—one of the older women in Irena's network—and her family's house was ideal because it had two entrances, one in the front and one in the back garden. Two ways in and out was crucial to have in an underground station. Lekarska Street—where the house fronted—was also divided down the middle and strung with barbed wire. On the opposite side of the street, the Polish residents had been turned out to make room for German doctors and nurses who worked at the nearby *Volksdeutsche* hospital. On the other side lived Polish families like Jaga's.

The Germans, Jaga told friends with a laugh, were such an orderly, rule-following people, that they couldn't imagine anyone would do something as outrageously brazen as have fifty Jewish people coming and going in front of them. The Gestapo expected the resistance to be covert. But, like Maria Palester's family, Jaga was hiding in the open.

A man had been murdered in the neighborhood—it may have been a targeted resistance assassination—and the German soldiers were doing searches of the Polish houses, door by door, looking for their suspect. Patrols blocked both ends of the street to keep anyone from escaping. The pounding feet and barked orders worked their way toward the middle—where Jaga's house stood. She and her family were surrounded. There was no sneaking out the back exit. When the Nazis came to the house and started searching, Jaga could try to bluff, but the Jewish people would be recognized for who they were. And there was no question about what would happen. The penalty for hiding a Jew was death—death for the entire family.

Jaga paced barefoot in the kitchen, cold with terror. *Her daughter. Her parents. How could she save them?* The shouts on the streets closed in, and Jaga whispered a prayer, the words of the Hail Mary. One of the children watched, wide-eyed. *It's all because we are Jewish.* His solemn assessment of the situation rattled Jaga.

*The poor child.* If these Jewish children died unbaptized, their souls would be lost to God forever. Jaga, a devout Catholic, turned to those around her. In moments of *extremis*—when death was imminent—the baptism ritual could be performed by any one of the faithful. A priest was not required for the sacrament.

Jaga heard German shouts outside in the street. She pondered only a moment before deciding to baptize the Jews hiding with her. As her mother and her daughter looked on, as the tromp of boots echoed closer, she turned to the water jug. Gesturing to show them how to make the sign of the cross, Jaga baptized them. The Jewish child looked up at her and sighed. "So now we are just like the others?"

Jaga hugged the child, knowing their baptism would mean nothing to the Germans. She fell to her knees to pray in the front of the kitchen stove, and the Jewish refugees knelt beside her on the kitchen floor to pray. And they waited for the soldiers.

Poised near the fire burning in the stove, Jaga clutched a bit of paper in her hand. The newest list of Irena's children and the places they were hidden. When the Germans knocked, she would toss it into the flames. Then she would try to die with courage. Until then, Jaga keep praying. The murmur of prayer filled the room, and it came to Jaga suddenly. *The sounds of the soldiers were fading. The Germans were leaving!*

The search squads met in the middle of the block in front the Jaga's home. Each thought the other had searched it. The Germans left Lekarska Street without ever knocking.

The fate Jaga's family and their guests escaped became obvious. In the manhunt that morning, the Nazis found five Jewish men in a home near Jaga's. All five and the entire Polish family hiding them were shot dead at the crossroad.

# 14

## The Ghetto Uprising

### Ala Gołab-Grynberg—Spring 1943

Passover eve fell on April 18, 1943, and throughout the quarter, despite meager provisions, families prepared to celebrate. Before midnight, Ala heard rumors that the Nazis planned an *Aktion* for the day of Passover. Everyone in the ghetto believed such rumors after all the death they'd seen in the *Aktions* last year. People abandoned their scanty feast tables and started packing. Not for the east. Not for desperate flight across the ghetto wall. But to take refuge in hidey-holes, in hidden attic rooms, and in belowground bunkers they had spent the spring building.

Ala had survived these long, desperate months by working as a seamstress in Toebbens's factory, but that was not her calling. Amid the ruins of the Jewish hospital, where Ala lived in a crumbling basement at number 4 Gesia Street, she and Nachum Remba joined once again with other nurses and doctors to set up a makeshift emergency medical point. Ala's nursing skills would soon be needed. The remnant of Jews still alive in the ghetto would not submit to another round of deportations.

Word spread throughout the district. The time had come to make a stand. While the children and the frail took refuge, the young people climbed the rooftops and took up posts in the alleys. Scouts manned observation posts and reviewed the codes for passing messages. By 2:30 a.m. the resistance had mobilized nearly 750 armed young men and women. Everyone in the ghetto watched and waited for dawn.

Near 6 a.m., the sun rose, casting brilliant rays over the far horizon. When the sky lightened, ghetto gates awakened with the noise of engines firing to life. SS tanks and artillery motorcycle units and soldiers swept into the district. Unseen Jewish fighters crept into position, cutting off the path of retreat behind the SS. Armed with revolvers, homemade bombs, and a handful of rifles, the Jewish resistance struck hard and fast.

The attack blew up tanks and columns of Nazi troops, catching the Germans by surprise. As the battle raged through the day, Jewish fighters prevailed over the superior SS forces, and ghetto dwellers went wild with jubilation. Around 5 p.m., the stunned Germans withdrew.

The streets fell silent. The ghetto ground was strewn with dead. Some two hundred resistance fighters, and even more Germans, perished. Old men came from their hiding places to kiss the cold cheeks of the young heroes lying motionless on the sidewalks. Strangers embraced and cried with joy. Ala knew the celebration would be short-lived, but this moment felt good after years of brutal suppression.

The following day, the Germans did not return until early afternoon. The fierce fight took up as before. A cheer went up as the ghetto fighters killed a hundred Germans at once with a strategically placed mine. Fearless teenage girls, with nothing to lose, carried hand grenades hidden in their underpants up to the last moment, when they were near enough to make the explosion count.

Ala used her few remaining bandages and medicines to help the injured, and she continued to coordinate with Irena to save people from German hands. For the first few days, when the Germans were too distracted to worry about a few Polish women, Irena and Irka Schultz made some reckless forays into the ghetto, passes or no.

## On the Aryan Side

Warm weather welcomed Holy Week in Warsaw that spring. A carnival popped up Palm Sunday like a gaudy flower, on the Aryan side of the ghetto wall. It featured a "sky-carrousel" that lifted young and old alike high in the air. Young Polish courting couples fancied the time at the top of the wheel. Between kisses they caught long, slow-motion glimpses into the forbidden Jewish Quarter. Below, they enjoyed hot pastries peddled by vendors. Long into the evening carnival music blended with the squeals of children's laughter.

The carnival music played on while SS troops surged into the ghetto to battle the Jewish fighters. Irena's contacts at Żegota mobilized support for the resistance from the outside, carrying weapons and explosives through tunnels dug beneath the ghetto walls.

Irena received a message and scurried to meet the Żegota agents and try to help. Arriving breathless at the secret apartment serving as Żegota headquarters, she heard Easter church bells ringing out across the city. Women floated past in holiday hats and flower print dresses. From the open windows came the sounds of families sitting down to their joyous Easter breakfast.

She went inside to find that the latest reports contained bad news from the ghetto fighters. The Germans responded to the Jewish uprising by setting fire to buildings one by one and forcing people out of hiding. Smoke poured over the walls, the breeze carrying large flakes of gray white ash into the springtime air over central Warsaw.

Beating the Germans had been impossible from the start, and now the task had become helping any survivors who managed to flee with their lives. They needed safe places to go. Her friend Julian, the chief of Żegota, told Irena, ". . . help them. Give me some addresses where we can take people who make it to the Aryan side."

Irena drew up a list of the locations of her emergency rooms where Jews would be safe, including her own apartment. And she could count on Jaga and her sister Janka. "Żegota [sent] the addresses of apartments we called 'emergency rooms,'" she explained, "and where people who had decided to flee the ghetto could show up."

The burning of the ghetto could be clearly seen from Swietojerska Street and from Krasinski Square, and there, despite it all, the carnival continued. Irena worried about Ala. She stood at the wall each day, wracking her brain for a way to support Ala, to let her know she was thinking of her. She tried to get in and find her, but the Germans barred the ghetto gates to everyone. Her ghetto pass was useless. Of all her prewar Jewish friends, only Ala remained inside the walls. Irena could do nothing to help her.

Irena considered further. She knew it was a daring risk—even more daring than some of their old operations. But if the Germans were hell-bent on destruction street by street, Irena spotted opportunity. She wondered: Were the Germans distracted enough that she could perhaps get back into the ghetto? And if she could get in, surely she could get out with some people? Irena made it in—and out again—that day, making contact with Ala, and brought a youngster to the Aryan side.

It could be done! She mobilized her team, and for the next few days the women were, once again, in and out of the ghetto. Irka Schultz fearlessly rushed into burning buildings and pulled out crying toddlers. Irena waited at sewer manholes and tunnel exits, directing refugees to safe house addresses. For a week or two, the ruse worked, and families crawled through the sewers to safety.

But soon, the Germans grew wise to the escape routes. They now shut off all the city utilities and pumped poison into the water and gas mains to kill those escaping.

## Janka Grabowska

On the Aryan side of the city, Janka received a frantic message from Regina Mikelberg. Surviving her jump from a cattle car headed to Treblinka, Regina had made her way back to Warsaw and now wanted to rescue her younger sister from the ghetto. The strong and healthy girl had been assigned to a work detail. When her group of factory workers were herded to the *Umschlagplatz* and sent away on the trains, Regina's sister survived by concealing herself beneath a pile of corpses for several days. But now, the girl needed to get out of the ghetto. Her luck would not stretch forever. Janka was a friend of the Mikelberg family and had used her epidemic control pass to bring them food and medicine. Irena helped with the planning, but they agreed Janka would run this operation.

A gentle tap came at the back door as Janka prepared to leave. She opened the garden entrance to see her husband, Jozef, lying on the steps bleeding. He was a soldier in the Home Army and had been wounded on a mission. Janka hauled him over the threshold, out of the view of the neighbors. What to do now? Drive her husband to the hospital or keep her appointment in the ghetto?

Jozef gave a painful laugh when she explained the dilemma. *Wrap me up, Janka,* he said, before losing consciousness.

Janka made her husband as comfortable as possible and kissed him good-bye. He would have to hang on until she could get him a doctor tomorrow.

The rescue went off and Janka brought the frightened girl home with her that evening, but she couldn't stay. With Jozef here wounded, hiding someone was too much of a gamble. The Mikelberg sisters moved instead to a Jewish safe house run by Janka's mother, who was also part of Irena's far-flung network.

Word spread of underground cafés where Jews on the run could meet. Irena had post office drops throughout the city to leave messages if someone was in need of a safe house or an illegal doctor. There was a laundry where she left messages for couriers.

That spring, each day seemed to grow more dangerous for Jews hiding in Warsaw, and for anyone aiding them. Often the Gestapo's brutal interrogations succeeded, giving them evidence to make more arrests. One person captured and made to talk resulted in more raids and more opportunity to torture answers from people.

Irena's office mate, Stefania Wichlińksa, the woman who had introduced her to Żegota, was arrested April 4. Tortured for nearly a month, Stefania refused to reveal Irena's name. She was executed in the ruins of the ghetto, leaving a husband, Stefan, and two children.

## Ala Gołab-Grynberg

By early May, those left in the ghetto had almost no chance of escaping, and no firepower worth aiming at German planes that flew low and dropped bombs on the few apartment buildings still standing. Ala, Nachum, his wife, and other close friends retreated to bunkers and hideouts in the burnt-out buildings on Gesia Street, where they continued providing desperate residents and resistance fighters with medical services. Ala stowed away in a ground floor apartment at number 4 Gesia Street, next door to the old hospital buildings. Nachum and his wife were in a bunker across the street.

On May 8, the German patrols raided the bunkers on Gesia Street. All around Ala, the ghetto was burning. "There was no air, only black, choking smoke and heavy, burning heat radiating from the red-hot walls, from the glowing stone stairs. The flames cling to our clothes, which now start smoldering. The pavement melts under our feet," as one of Ala's friends described it.

Mothers jumped with their small children to their deaths four or five stories below, amid a hail of Nazi gunfire. Charred corpses lay on the streets, and buildings were reduced to rubble. In the underground dirt cellars, the hospital team crouched together fearfully, piling rocks carefully to hide from view their children. But the Nazis hunted with dogs now, and one of those dogs betrayed Ala. She could taste the dirt and ash in her mouth, and her legs trembled as she crawled out into the open at gunpoint.

Ala came out with her hands up. A soldier waved her into line with his gun, and she marched with the others to an assembly point at Nalewki Street. From there, every path led to the *Umschlagplatz*. In all these months had she known she would take her turn in a cattle car? Or had a spark of hope remained that she might live to join Rami and Arek? It didn't matter what she had believed.

In the two days they waited for the train to come, it was impossible to believe in anything good. German and Ukrainian soldiers brutalized young men, searching for hidden weapons. Ala tried not to watch as some girls were assaulted by a gang of laughing soldiers. Murmurs of pain or protest were silenced with iron cudgels. Long shadows fell across the dead when the soldiers corralled the survivors, driving them to the tracks, whipping, shoving. At last, the door rammed shut, iron scraping iron, skin pressing against skin, body crushing body, moans from low in the throat, cries rising, until there was no air and the thunder of the wheels on the track took everything away.

Jews led by the SS to the deportation trains at the end of the Jewish ghetto uprising, Spring 1943. *National Archives and Records Administration, College Park Instytut Pamieci Narodowej Zydowski Insty*

Jews marched to the *Umschlagplatz* at the end of the Jewish ghetto uprising, Spring 1943. *National Archives and Records Administration, College Park Instytut Pamieci Narodowej Zydowski Insty*

## Final Destruction of the Ghetto

As dusk settled over Warsaw on May 16, a colossal blast of dynamite shook the ghetto. The Great Synagogue trembled for a moment, and crumbled—the Nazis' final act of destruction, a symbol of their annihilation of Poland's Jews. The German governor-general of the city informed his superiors in Berlin, "Jews, bandits, and subhumans were destroyed. The Jewish Quarter of Warsaw is no more."

Only the bombed out steeple tower of St. Augustine's Church rose up forlornly in the center of a sea of concrete and brick rubble. The governor-general proudly reported that the total number of Jews destroyed in the final *Aktion* totaled 56,065, out of a population of perhaps 60,000."

Only a handful of the Warsaw ghetto fighters escaped the burning ghetto and transport to the camps. These fighters, fewer than two hundred, managed to slip, undetected, to the Aryan side in the last days of the revolt. Ala's friend Marek Edelman was one of them. Later he remembered the ghetto collapsing around them, a few strong and lucky men and women "half-walked, half-crawled for twenty hours" through sewers booby-trapped by the Germans, squeezing themselves through fetid pipes just over two feet tall in darkness. On the other side, trucks and comrades awaited, ready to rush them away to the forests or safe houses. At one of those grates, Irena stood sentinel.

# 15

## Gestapo Raid

### Betrayed

Brackiej Street was just off a main thoroughfare to the east of where the ghetto had stood, and its busy storefronts included a laundry shop where housewives could get some relief, if they had the money to spare. Women came and went all day picking up neatly wrapped brown paper parcels or weekly linens in baskets. Sometimes certain women came and went bringing other items, tucked among the folds of garments.

In October of 1943, the Gestapo arrested the woman who ran the shop, accusing her of aiding the resistance in passing parcels and messages. Taken to Szucha Avenue and tortured, brutalized at Pawiak, and interrogated again with iron bars and truncheons, the broken woman gave the Gestapo all the information she knew. She was almost certainly executed afterward. But a person could not be blamed for naming names. No one knew whether they would be able to withstand torture. When the laundry owner cracked, she named at least three women who used her shop as an underground mailbox. One of them was Irena Sendler.

## October 19, 1943

By that fall, the deprivation, terror, and murderous brutality of Nazi occupation had ground its heel on Warsaw through four long years. Irena kept hope burning by focusing on "her" children, doing all she could to keep them alive and safe. But nightmares troubled her sleep, and ghosts shadowed her days. The absence of so many people she had loved painfully weighed upon her. Ala, Ewa, Rachela, Jozef, Dr. Korczak and his precious girls and boys . . . all gone.

It was necessary to hold close those who remained, and so on Irena's name day, the Feast of St. Irena, friends and family gathered for a small party. After cake and cordials, Irena's mother and an aunt who'd come to stay went to bed. But Irena and Janka stayed up talking long after curfew. They had their share of perilous moments in their underground resistance work, but Janka had an irreverent sense of humor and could make Irena laugh. They didn't settle down to sleep on their makeshift beds in the living room until 2 a.m.

They would be up early. Irena had a list of children to

visit in the morning, Jewish children with fake Polish identities. As always, before she went to bed, she placed her precious lists of children's names and addresses in the center of the kitchen table, underneath the window. She tucked her weathered work bag, full of blank identity papers and a large sum of money, near her bed for safekeeping. Then she fell asleep.

A noise awakened Irena, and her mother cried out in alarm. Next she heard pounding on the door. A few precious moments passed before sleep cleared from Irena's head and she jumped up.

"Open! Gestapo!" More battering against the door. Then came a loud scratch at the wood and the scream of the door cracking.

Irena grabbed the lists from the table as she had practiced many times. She felt calm; she had prepared for this moment. Sailing toward the window, reaching to push the papers to the garden, she froze. Gestapo agents looked up at her from below. A few choice words escaped her lips. Her calm vanished. As she scanned the room, the pounding and shouting grew more furious and the door threatened to give way. The tissue paper turned moist in her hand. "It's the lists of children." She tossed them to Janka. "Hide it." Irena's voice was hoarse. "Don't let them find it!"

She had time to see Janka stuff the list into her bra before the door shattered open. Gestapo swarmed in.

Behind them Irena saw the horror-stricken face of Mr. Przeździecki, the building manager.

The agents towered over Irena, screaming threats and orders. She said nothing, and they started tearing apart the furniture. They ripped out the insides of the stove, pulled up the floorboards, threw dishes from the cupboards. Irena counted eleven of the men, trying to terrorize her. It worked. Her limbs shook, her heart stopped and then raced by turns.

She watched in horror and then awe as the men ripped open the mattress of her makeshift bed. Her bag full of identity documents and cash sat in plain sight. As they searched the mattress, the rickety bed frame collapsed on the bag, hiding it. The dreaded secret police had hidden from themselves the most incriminating evidence. But their destruction, their search went on . . . and on . . . and on. The sky outside turned light and still the brutes keep hunting.

All the while, they pummeled the other women with questions. Irena at last convinced the agents that Janka was an innocent out-of-town visitor like her aunt, although Janka was practically a neighbor. Her mother, the agents could see, was too ill to be engaged in the underground. That left Irena.

By 6 a.m., the agents decided there was nothing in the apartment to find. They did not find the list of Irena's children. An officer growled at Irena to get dressed, and be quick about it. Pulling on her skirt in a rush and trying to quickly button up a sweater, Irena's heart felt light. They were done searching. They hadn't discovered the lists. And if they didn't suspect Janka, they didn't know about her sister Jaga's apartment. Her gaze met Janka's, but she did not risk a smile. Now, if they could just get out of the apartment. . . .

The agents led her into the corridor and down the stairs, their heavy boots echoing in the stairwell. Irena pictured her neighbors listening at their doors. Soon the gossip would fly.

A prison van waited outside, the engine running. Irena saw Janka dash from the building and down the walkway. *What was she thinking?* In Janka's hands, Irena saw her shoes. *She will need them,* Janka said. *Please.* The men nodded, bored, and gestured for Irena to get on with it.

The doors slammed closed, and the prison van lurched into motion to Aleja Szucha. Irena supposed she had always known this would happen, but she wasn't prepared for it. Maybe one never was.

Irena must not show fear. The Nazis must not suspect she was hiding anything. That would only make what was coming harder to endure. But she was frightened. Very frightened. There were no words more terrifying than "Aleja Szucha, Szucha Avenue." There may have been no words more terrifying in all of wartime Europe.

The address of Warsaw's Gestapo headquarters was

25 Szucha Avenue. The building's imposing exterior suited the Germans' cruel purpose. Inside, corridors echoed with the screams of prisoners being questioned. Those who survived remembered the rank scent of fear and urine, the bloodstained cells and implements of torture.

As the van swayed round each street corner, Irena had time to think about her own trouble. They would kill her. She had always known the risks. People did not return from Aleja Szucha, or from Pawiak, the prison where detainees stayed locked up in between their bone-crushing interrogations. They did not return from camps like Auschwitz or Ravensbrück, where the innocent prison "survivors" were deported. And Irena Sendler was not innocent. The Gestapo had just captured one of the most important figures in the Polish underground. Irena could only hope that the Germans did not know it.

The van cranked hard to the right, heading southeast across the still sleeping city, passing the ruin of the ghetto, its rubble a killing ground, an endless graveyard, where she'd last seen Ala. Ala Gołab-Grynberg disappeared in that final inferno when the Nazi's destroyed the ghetto. There were whispers in the underground that Ala was still alive, in the German labor camp at Poniatowa, with others in the Jewish resistance, secretly planning an escape. Irena hoped it was true, prayed Ala would return when this awful war ended to collect her small daughter, Rami, from the orphanage where Irena had hidden her.

The sun had still to rise over Warsaw, and in the morning half-light, the agents closest to her dozed. Irena forced herself into some state of calm and tried to think rationally. Janka knew how important the lists were—and how dangerous. She would hide them. If the Nazis got their hands on them, they'd launch a series of executions. The Gestapo would hunt down the Jewish children and murder the Polish men and women carefully tending and shielding the little ones. They would kill Irena's mother, even though the frail, bedridden woman could only guess at the extent of her daughter's shadowy activities. Irena couldn't help but feel that she had been a bad daughter. She had always been, she knew, more like her impetuous, idealist father.

If the lists were lost or Janka destroyed them as a safety measure, that, too, would cause problems. When Irena died there would be no one to reconstruct them. Only she knew what was written on the thin slips of paper. She had promised mothers and fathers who went to the Treblinka extermination camp that she would tell their children who they were and that their parents had loved them. When Irena was dead, there would be no one able to keep that promise.

As the van turned south toward the broad boulevards, Irena thought of Dr. Radlinska and her dozens of other sleeping conspirators scattered across the city. At least she hoped they were sleeping and not in vans like this, riding to Szucha Avenue. There was no point in pretending.

What was coming would be terrible. She knew that. *Was there pain enough in the world that would lead her to betray her friends? The children?*

Irena thought she could bear it. But most could not stand the torture. She must steel her nerves. She would die in silence. As long as her friends and the children survived, she told herself she could suffer anything. But that was what everyone said at the beginning.

The morning felt cold, and her fear icy. Whatever came next would be far more chilling. As they approached the final turn, Irena slipped her hands into her coat pockets for some brief comfort. A jolt like electricity. She choked off a yelp. Her hand closed around the small roll of cigarette paper covered with the names of children whose support funds she planned to deliver this morning. She'd forgotten last night to take it out of her jacket.

Irena rode a rising tide of panic. They neared Szucha. She had very little time. She shredded the tissue paper in her pocket. Its flimsy texture gave way. At least it would smudge the writing. The agent nearest her swayed with the van's motion, his head bobbing. He appeared to be sleeping. What else could she do but this one last gamble? She lifted her hand gently to the open window and let the tiny scraps flutter free. The agent turned, snorted, then nothing. Irena leaned back in the broad seat and closed her eyes, too. But that didn't stop her tears.

*The slaughterhouse.* That's what people called the squat

gray compound on Szucha Avenue. Steel chains and locks studded the iron gates that rose up before them. The guards wore high black boots with a glossy polish, and ugly whips slung from their belts. A bored officer hustled Irena into the building. Beyond the doorway, she could make out a large interrogation room. But they pushed her along into a small room, where a typewriter clacked, and the radio played German music while she gave her name and address.

Then they led her into another room where a tall German man with a smooth gentle manner asked her questions in perfect Polish. *What was her name? Where did she live? Who was her family?* They were easy questions. The Gestapo already knew the answers. Irena understood the game they played, how they hoped she would let down her guard.

Soon enough, the questions led Irena onto more perilous ground. *We know you are helping the resistance and the Jews. What organization are you working for? It will go better for you.* They knew names of the Żegota leadership. They knew about the underground post-box at the laundry. The thickness of the man's file was the most frightening thing yet.

Irena relaxed her face, allowing none of her fear to show. *I know nothing,* she said. *This is all a misunderstanding. I'm a social worker. Naturally, that brings me into contact with many people. If someone in my circle is doing anything illegal, I know nothing of it.*

The Gestapo officer gave her a thin smile and arched an eyebrow. She read his wordless meaning. He had seen it all before. Everyone protested their innocence in the beginning. But here on Aleja Szucha, they had ways.

*So be it, Pani Sendler.* "Pani" was the word for "ma'am" in Polish. There wasn't a loose thread on his impeccable uniform. Everything acquiesced to this man. *We will talk further,* he said. *I promise.*

Afterward, a guard pushed Irena along the corridor. The tunes still drifted from the wireless, but at this early hour, everything else was quiet. The corridor narrowed, and ceilings dropped low. Irena passed four cells, each with iron grates and a row of thin wooden benches. A cell door pushed open. Inside prisoners slumped on the benches. None took notice of Irena's stumbling entrance. *Sit. No moving. Keep your eyes on the back of the head in front of you. No speaking.* Irena smelled fear in the damp cell. She had joined the others arrested last night, all sleepless and scared.

Sitting on the hard, low bench was uncomfortable. Irena had to buck up. This would be the best of what would come. The ground beneath her shoe felt sticky. *Blood.* A wave of dizziness flooded over her. She breathed deep and sat motionless with the others, for how long, she couldn't guess.

Soon, the guards brought groups of prisoners and the benches filled. The wireless music stopped, leaving only the sound of footsteps echoing in the passageway and soft weeping. One by one, the guards called names and led prisoners away. Thumps, whacks, and thuds punctuated Irena's thoughts, followed by screams, more screams, and occasional gunshots.

Agony resounded from upper floors and the basement beneath, flowing through open doors and windows. Purposefully left open doors and windows were an incentive to those waiting their turn.

Prisoners soon distinguished a pattern in the noises: curt questions, murmured answers, piercing questions, louder answers, a smack, or a blow, a shriek, a woman's sob. Irena shivered in her sweat-drenched clothes and tried to think of other things. Anything but the torture that awaited her.

Maybe in those long hours her thoughts drifted to happy moments from her childhood. Due to the generosity of a rich uncle, Irena and her family had lived in a spacious villa in Otwock. As a young child, she had the run of twenty rooms, one of them a glass solarium that sparkled in the sunshine. When she pictured her papa, his handlebar mustache curling high when he smiled, that made her happy. Though an educated man, he treated everyone as his equal. Her mother was a friendly, outgoing woman, and so their large, square house at number 21 Kościuszk Street often filled with guests.

She was an only child and her papa had lavished her

with affection. She remembered her aunts scolding when he gave her hugs and kisses. The aunts would tell him, "Don't spoil her, Stasiu. What will become of her?" Her father had winked and hugged her closer. He told the aunts, "We don't know what her life will be like. Maybe my hugs will be her best memory."

The Gestapo interrogators beat Irena badly that first day. That was just the normal practice on the first day at Szucha. When prisoners did not give the desired answers, they got fists to the face, boots to the ribs, bone-shattering blows with rubber truncheons and burns from hot irons.

Taken back to their cells, the limp and bloodied inmates were ordered to sit at attention until the prison trucks arrived to transport them to Pawiak prison for the night. Inside the darkness of the transport truck that afternoon, Irena tried to deny the pain of her bruised and bleeding body. She pushed away at her fear. The truck sped across the city, its horn blowing a mournful refrain, and Irena tried to banish all thought of the future. But a swirl of fear closed in, her body constricting with relentless pain.

# 16

## Pawiak Prison

**Winter 1943–1944**

When the truck reached Pawiak prison, guards hauled off inmates unable to walk. A handful of grim-faced nurses and doctors pulled the most badly beaten from the truck and loaded them onto canvas army stretchers. A guard herded Irena down broad stone stairs. Arriving inside the prison, it was clear the only way out of here was death. It was just a matter of quick or slow.

But a prisoner could find small comforts here. Locked in her cell that night, Irena discovered a woman who'd once lived in her Wola apartment building. Basia Dietrich grasped Irena's hands in the darkness, and they shared a whispered, urgent conversation, long after lights-out. Basia had been a scout leader and ran the community kindergarten. She also served as a captain in the resistance, running an operation similar to Irena's network rescuing Jewish children.

At 9 a.m. each morning, the prison guards called roll. One list of prisoners boarded vans and rolled out of the yard toward Szucha for further interrogation. Another list of people climbed into trucks headed to an execution site in the burned-out Jewish ghetto. Irena heard her name called on a list of patients ordered to visit the medical clinic. Irena recognized the woman reading off the names. Jadwiga Jedrzejowska had been a student of Dr. Radlinska's several years ahead of Irena. She'd disappeared in 1942, after a roundup of people working in the underground press. To her surprise, Irena heard Jadwiga call out her name on the roster of women scheduled to visit the prison dentist, even though her teeth had survived her first day of torture intact.

When Irena arrived for her appointment, the dentist turned out to be Dr. Anna Sipowicz, another acquaintance from her prewar activist days. As she waited, Irena stared out the window of Anna's cramped office, which offered a sobering view of the ghetto ruins. Then Anna gestured her toward the dental chair and, in hushed tones, explained the dental procedure would not fix a tooth. Rather, Anna would drill a hole and stuff it with a wad of tissue paper, on which a message had been written. Then she asked Irena, *Is there any message you need to send?*

Irena nodded. On tissue-thin paper, she wrote, "The lists are safe!" The people in her network would be frantic.

Pawiak prison, where Irena and many of her friends were incarcerated by the Gestapo. *Yad Vashem*

If the lists had been discovered, they must move the children right away. Żegota needed to know the Gestapo had not found the names and addresses.

Irena returned to her cell and extracted the message from her tooth. The message said, "We are doing everything we can to get you out of that hell." With her arrest, Irena had turned into a threat against her entire organization and all of the children she had helped save. Her Żegota conspirators had to encourage her to be strong, to withstand her torture and not give up information to the Nazis.

## Ala Gołab-Grynberg

Ala could not know that her dear friend had been arrested, just as Irena could not know that Ala was still alive in a labor camp at Poniatowa, in the Lublin district, slaving for the Germans. She had not died in the Treblinka showers like 85 percent of the Jews from the Warsaw ghetto. Baby Bieta's mother, Henia Koppel, was also alive and laboring as a seamstress at the camp, where fifteen thousand Jews worked for German war profiteers Toebbens and Shultz, the same men who had exploited them in the ghetto. But the resistance movement was growing in the camp. A number of the people, shipped in from Warsaw, like Ala, had been participants or fighters in the Warsaw ghetto uprising.

In late October, camp guards suddenly broke routine,

took prisoners off their regular jobs, manufacturing prod-
ucts including floor tiles and German uniforms, and sent
them to work in fields near the camp. Prodded by guards,
whipped, threatened at gunpoint, the men and women
dug trenches, two meters wide and two meters deep. The
long, zigzagging excavations, they were told, were air-raid
defense trenches. Work went on for days, and word was,
next they would build air-raid towers.

But Ala and others in the resistance didn't believe it,
and they became watchful and alert. They had a small arse-
nal of weapons, smuggled into the camp with the help of
Żegota, and when the Germans ordered a dawn roll call of
all prisoners the morning of November 4, Ala knew, with
a sinking heart, something terrible was coming. The resistance leaders—men and women—huddled and quickly
made a bold decision. They would not report for roll call.
They gathered, instead, in one of the barracks and set up
barricades, ready for defensive military action. The cache
of weapons was tiny, but these were men and women who
had seen firsthand the Nazis' merciless slaughter.

Along the trenches, in freezing weather, the Nazis
called the prisoners forward in groups of fifty. At gunpoint,
guards forced them to strip off their clothing and set their
valuables into small baskets. Then they walked the Jewish
people to the trenches, forced them to lie down, group by
group, in layers, and shot them one by one.

Henia Koppel was twenty-four years old when she

died in one of the trenches. Bieta was now an orphan. But Ala did not die lying down with the others. She had spent half of her thirty-nine years nursing people, trying to keep them alive, healthy, and what mother did not yearn to live, to see her daughter grow up? Ala had long been fierce and fearless. When the guards and their dogs came for her and the others banding together in the barracks, Ala would not be taken. The resistance fighters opened fire on the SS, shooting guards to the ground. The casualties stunned the German officers, but they quickly regained their purpose and attacked the prisoners. When the Jewish fighters refused to come out, guards set the barracks afire. Ala and her friends, trapped in the blaze, died, fighting to the bitter end. In those final hellish moments, as the world exploded in flames around her, Ala surely thought of her husband, Arek, perhaps still somewhere out there fighting, and her small daughter in hiding.

The executions in the field outside Poniatowa continued for two days. Of the fifteen hundred prisoners, three escaped the trenches and survived. In the same two-day period, the Germans also executed Jewish prisoners at two other slave labor camps, finally reporting to superiors they had exterminated every Jew in the Lublin district, some forty-three thousand men, women, and children. The Nazis code-named this massive murder operation *Erntefest*—"harvest festival."

. . .

Some mornings in Pawaik, Irena heard her name called to board the transport to *Szucha*. Each evening, she returned to prison more broken than before. The Gestapo interrogators disfigured women with cigarette burns and mutilated them with penknives and cigarette burns. Often women died under torture.

Irena wondered, *How long could she bear the pain? Would she die to save the others?* Under questioning, she repeated her story over and over. Some days, she had enough concentration to float away from her poor, miserable body. Other times, the fierce beatings mercifully swept her unconscious. Twice a day, at noon and in the evening, the vans carted mangled bodies back to Pawiak.

The van had the air of an ambulance carrying victims of a disaster. Pale faces covered in blood, black eyes, and soiled clothing. Some had to be supported by their companions or slid off the truck. Others had to be carried. Over time, Irena found herself in each of those categories.

Several weeks after her arrest, in mid-November, she caught sight of a bruised and obviously tortured Helena Szeszko in a cell at Pawiak. Helena was a nurse in the medical underground whom Ala had drawn into Irena's network. She'd organized medical hideouts for Irena's children who needed medical care. Under the code name Sonia, she had delivered Jewish children to Waldyslawa Marynowska for safekeeping at the Father Boduen orphanage.

Would Helena be strong? If not, Irena Schultz, Jadwiga

Deneka, and Waldyslawa Marynowska would be dead—and perhaps hundreds of children in the orphanages. Helena and Irena exchanged a careful glance when the women were herded to the courtyard for daily walks, or at meals shared a look of solidarity and determination.

In late November, another friend of Irena's showed up in prison. Jadwiga Deneka had been captured visiting a Jewish basement hideout and underground press distribution point in Warsaw's Żoliborz district.

The Germans treated twenty-four-year-old Jadwiga especially harshly because they believed that she was Jewish. As one of Irena's earliest partners, Jadwiga's first concern at Pawiak was using the prison network to smuggle out warnings and messages to those in her cell, urging them to go into hiding.

Irena's brutal questioning did not let up. By January, she hobbled on broken legs and feet. Leather whips, interwoven with strands of steel wire, left ugly open wounds running in jagged strips across her body. She suffered mental agony, as painful as her physical abuse.

The only reason she remained alive, that she had not been beaten to death, was that the Germans did not know whom they had captured. The Gestapo believed she was a small player, a foolish young woman dabbling at the periphery of the Polish resistance. They had not discovered her leadership role, nor that she was responsible for saving thousands of Jewish children. The torture used on small players in the Polish underground did not compare to the savage cruelty dealt to known resistance leaders.

When she wasn't being tortured Irena had an assigned job. She worked in the prison laundry, standing long hours on broken legs that could not heal properly. Propping herself on the sink, she scrubbed feces from stained Nazi underwear. When the laundry work did not satisfy the Germans, the workers endured sadistic punishment. One afternoon a guard lined the laundry women up against the wall, walked down the row, and put a bullet through the head of every other person. Irena came up lucky and survived.

At Pawiak, the women did their best to keep their spirits up, despite the hunger and regular physical abuse, despite the daily terror of erratic executions. Each morning they woke with the knowledge that it might be their last day alive. To pass empty hours, some of the women crafted playing cards or dolls from bread and bits of paper. In the evenings, when the guards had gone, the cells might fill with the sound of women singing sad Polish songs, children's lullabies, or old folk tunes. Irena and Basia slept crammed together, with a dozen or more others, in a small dank cell. Basia had one of the most beautiful voices. Listening to her was a taste of freedom.

One night Basia leaned against the cool cell wall and turned her face away. Irena guessed her friend was crying.

*Basia, what's the matter? Shall we sing something?*

Basia shook her head. A moment passed and she whispered, *Irena, they will execute me tomorrow. I have a feeling.* Irena whispered words of reassurance, but Basia stopped her.

*No. We saw Zbigniew Łapiński today. Coming out of the chapel. He had been beaten.* Zbigniew was a courier in the children's underground, only eighteen, a boy. Basia had watched the guards drag him limp and broken along the corridor after interrogation, and she'd spoke before thinking. She berated the young German lieutenant. *I gave away that we knew him, Irena.*

All that night, Irena lay awake and looked at the ceiling. Next to her, she knew that Basia couldn't sleep either. As they left the cell for roll call at dawn, Basia grasped Irena's hand and squeezed. The names were read out for the morning execution. *Basia Dietrich.* Irena heard her friend's name as if from a long way off. She tried not to cry there in front of the Germans. Basia and Zbigniew were executed that day in a public firing squad at the corner of Ordynacka and Foksal streets.

Irena went through Basia's last possessions in the cell that night, and her hand fell upon a small keepsake. A handmade portrait of Christ, with the words "I trust in Jesus." Irena held it close and let her tears flow.

On January 6, the name called was Jadwiga Deneka. In the ruins of the ghetto, just beyond the prison gates,

Jadwiga was executed alongside the eleven Jewish women she had been caught hiding. She had told nothing. Soon, Irena knew, it would be her turn.

Days later, Irena heard her name called in the morning lineup for another dental appointment. In the chair, as the drill buzzed, Anna Sipowicz handed Irena a message from Żegota. It no longer spoke of escape or freedom. It read, *Be strong. We love you.*

On the morning of January 20, 1944, in Pawiak prison, Irena heard her name called for the last time.

# 17

## Execution

### Warsaw, January 20, 1944

When Irena heard her name called for execution, the first thing she felt was relief. *No more torture. No more worry that she would crack under pressure and betray the children.* Shock followed close behind, a mixture of disbelief and panic.

Irena was one of twenty, perhaps thirty women, marched to the truck waiting in the prison yard. They would be driven to face the firing squad at Szucha.

The truck hauling inmates to their death had earned the name "the hood." A sturdy canvas cover stretched over top, blocking the prisoners from looking out and heightening their mounting sense of terror. The women jounced along in the dark, together in their shared fate, yet alone in facing death. The time neither sped nor slowed; it was simply the last minutes of life ticking away.

At the Gestapo headquarters, Irena and the others climbed out of the truck and were led into a waiting room. Some women cried softly, others sobbed loudly, a number of them remained stoic. Again, names were called. One after another, the woman named was led through a door on the left. One after another, volleys of gunfire rang out. The orderliness of the process started to fray. Women were bawling when Irena heard her name called.

The short walk across the room felt like falling . . . falling . . . falling. The world narrowed to Irena's footsteps and thoughts of her mother. She faced the door on the left, but the guard signaled her to take a door on the right. Momentary confusion turned to dread. *No. No more torture. She was ready to die.* She'd known it would come, and now she wanted it done.

In the room she entered, a Gestapo officer stood in his tall black boots, a sturdy German. *Come with me,* he said. Irena followed him out into the winter sunlight. Would he shoot her at the crossroads, like so many others? Her poorly healed legs hurt as she kept pace behind him, and then at the corner of Aleja Wyzwolenia and Aleja Szucha, the German said, "You are free. Save yourself fast."

Irena's brain stumbled over the meaning of his words. *Free? But she needed papers. Everyone needed identity papers in occupied Warsaw.*

"My *kennkarte*. I need my *kennkarte*," Irena told the German officer. "Give me my papers!"

The German's eyes flashed with rage. "You lousy thug, get lost," he snarled, smashing his fist into her mouth.

Irena staggered, dizzy. Her mouth filled with blood. She could not run on her injured legs. She hobbled a few steps, then a few more. She dragged herself into the nearest shop. A drugstore. A woman led her into a back room and helped her wash. The woman said her name was Helena. She bathed Irena's bloodied face and found some clothes to cover the prison uniform Irena wore. Helena gave her a few pennies to buy a tram ticket.

Irena's escape from death started to sink in. The city sights and sounds became real. Still, a fog of pain and shock dulled her mind. She stood at the tram stop, not knowing what to do. She would go home. Home to her mother. Irena boarded the number five tram with that single thought in her mind. She took a seat and the car rattled and swayed along the tracks.

A sudden cry panicked the passengers. *Gestapo at the next stop! Get off! Quick!* They were checking papers. The crowd rushed past, but Irena was half crippled and moving slowly. An old man stopped for a moment to help her down the steps. Irena limped into a crowd of pedestrians, trying to stay on her feet fighting back tears. Every part of her body hurt. She gritted her teeth against the pain and forced her mangled legs to keep moving. It was hours before she saw the familiar buildings of her street. By the time she hauled herself up the stairs to her mother's apartment, she could hardly stand.

For a day and night, Irena collapsed. As she gained strength she realized it was foolish to stay in the apartment where the Gestapo had arrested her. Her name appeared on notices around Warsaw, lists of people who'd been executed. In the streets, bullhorns blared the names of those murdered for crimes against Germany, and the news was posted on flyers. Irena read her own name among them. Sooner or later, someone who thought she'd been executed would realize she was alive, and the Gestapo would be back.

Staying was too dangerous. But leaving was impossible. Irena realized her mother was dying. She had suffered for years with a heart condition, and Irena's imprisonment had caused her mother much anxiety, worsening her condition. Irena felt responsible for her mother's weakening health. So she delayed leaving. A cousin had come to stay with her mother during the months of Irena's incarceration and promised to stay on. But Irena couldn't bear to leave her mother, and arranged to stay with a neighbor in the building, which allowed her to slip up the stairs for a few minutes every day and see her mother.

It was a foolish gamble. One night after 8 p.m. curfew, the tread of heavy boots sounded in the building, followed by the familiar German shouting. They had come for her again. They were searching the building. Irena heard cries and sounds of doors slamming on the first floor. She whirled, looking around the small apartment for a place to hide. *A closet? The bed?* There was no point in hiding. It was stupid to die like this. *Stupid.* She could not believe she had been so foolish. This time, she knew that it would kill her mother.

Minutes seemed an eternity. Irena waited breathless, her heart pounding—until the footsteps moved away, and in time the corridors grew quiet. There came a tap on the door. Irena's cousin had slipped down the staircase and brought Irena a note from her mother.

"They were looking for you again. You must not come near even to say good-bye to me. Get out as soon as possible."

The Gestapo had only searched the lower floors of the building. Had they gone up one more floor, they would have found Irena. Her mother was right. And the kindly neighbor's nerves were shattered. Żegota arranged new identity papers, and it was time for Irena to go into hiding just as she had sent thousands of others.

Żegota went to such length to free Irena—a single agent in a large and sprawling network with a hundred different cells—in largest part, because of the lists of children. Żegota knew from Irena's messages from prison that the Germans had not discovered the lists, but not that Janka had them.

This irony did not escape Irena. She had been keeping the lists to protect the children. But the lists saved her life.

Żegota knew if Irena died, the only trace of the children's Jewish families would die, too.

Irena realized in retrospect that tossing the lists out the window, no matter how many times she practiced the maneuver, had been naïve and foolish. What to do with the lists now? It was another pressing question, as members of their cell kept falling into the clutches of the Gestapo. Janka was still hiding the tissue rolls that Irena had tossed to her the morning of the arrest, but there were other parts of the list also stashed away for safekeeping. But what if Irena were again arrested? What if something happened to Janka? Janka's husband, Józef, was a resistance soldier in the Home Army, and their home was accordingly exposed and vulnerable. The lists needed to be gathered together and hidden properly. In the winter of 1944, Irena and sisters Janka and Jaga went in secret to Jaga's overgrown backyard on Lekarska Street and buried the lists of children's names in a soda bottle under the apple tree.

# 18

## Irena Goes Underground

**1944**

Irena was a hunted woman. When the Gestapo discovered her escape, they realized how important she must be in the resistance, and they would search until they found her. It was Irena's turn to memorize a new identity. She was Klara Dabrowska, who looked quite a lot like Irena Sendler, except for the dyed red hair. Her whereabouts was a strict secret. Initially, she went to a safe house in Otwock to recover from the trauma of Pawiak. There, friends told her the story behind her last minute rescue from the firing squad.

Right after her arrest, Żegota had agreed to supply money if a bribe could be arranged. The problem was finding someone with close contacts in the Gestapo. One could not just go up to a Nazi on the street and offer a bribe. The only person in the network with contacts among the

Germans was Maria Palester. Maria had continued her weekly bridge games, chatting up Gestapo informers. Through the years of Nazi occupation, she had developed an extensive network of contacts. Maria could call in her favors and reach out to offer a bribe, but it would be dangerous to deal with a high-ranking German at Gestapo headquarters.

Simply making contact would endanger Maria's life, and her family's. Henryk was no less Jewish than when the family had ignored orders to move to the ghetto. Her son, Krystof, was in the Polish resistance. And the family was helping hide Jewish friends Maria Proner and her daughter, Janina. But Maria was willing to risk it. Irena had helped her family survive, and if she could, she would save Irena. She reached out to a friend, who arranged the bribe with the German who had led Irena to the crossroads. Lured by a huge amount of money, he agreed to enter in the records that Irena Sendler had been executed.

But delivering the money was one more dangerous step. Malgorzata Palester, Maria and Henryk's fourteen-year-old daughter, agreed to do it. She carried rolls of cash buried in the bottom of her school backpack and went to meet the Gestapo agent. The amount of money was the highest ransom Żegota ever paid to save someone, in the neighborhood of thirty-five thousand zlotys (about one hundred thousand in today's dollars). The German might easily have taken the cash and shot Malgorzata. Or he might have taken the money and still led Irena to her execution, but he did what he'd agreed to do.

As Irena gained strength, she didn't want to sit still, and like some of the children she had rescued, she could not afford to. She had to keep moving, and she insisted on returning to her work in the underground, determined to continue checking in on her children and delivering funds for their keep. At one point, Irena hid at the Warsaw zoo, with some thirty Jewish people also taking safety there. This motley group of survivors called the zoo Noah's Ark.

Friends noticed Irena had changed. And who wouldn't fall into dark moments, after what she's endured in Pawiak prison? The nightmares that had haunted her even before her arrest grew worse after the months of physical and psychological torture.

Her mother was bedridden, her health deteriorating daily. Irena struggled with the notion she was a bad and selfish daughter. In hindsight, she saw that all along, her resistance work had endangered her mother's life. Now, her mother was dying and with the Gestapo searching for Irena, she could not risk visiting her mother—even for a few moments in the daytime. She felt she had betrayed her mother, and living on the lam as Klara, she grew lonely and isolated.

By March, Irena's mother was critically ill. Irena could not bear for her mother to die alone in her apartment, and she asked her old friend Dr. Majkowski to help smuggle her mother into hiding. They came up with the plan to whisk her mother away to a local hospital on a false emergency. An ambulance pulled up at her mother's apartment, and she was loaded in. The Gestapo men on surveillance gave chase, but a timely tie-up in traffic delayed them.

The ambulance arrived at the hospital and attendants wheeled Irena's mother to a room on an upper story of the building. In the few stolen moments before the Gestapo could locate her, nurses in the resistance helped the frail woman step out an open window and get down the fire escape. Another ambulance waited in the alley, engine running, ready to transport Irena's mother to a Żegota safe house. The safe house happened to be the apartment of Stefan Wichliński, widower of Stefania, the coworker who had first connected Irena with Żegota.

When the Gestapo arrived at the hospital, they found paperwork showing Irena's mother had been "transferred" to another clinic. But somehow, the details of that location were missing. Irena could now safely visit her mother, and was with her in her final moments on March 30, 1944. She had one last request of her daughter before she died. *Don't go to my funeral,* she begged Irena. *They will be looking for you there. Promise.* Irena promised.

And her mother was right. Friends at the funeral reported that a scowling Gestapo agent accosted friends and family. "Which is the dead woman's daughter?" Mourners shrugged. "Her daughter is in Pawiak prison."

"She certainly was," came the tight-lipped reply, "but she inexplicably isn't any longer."

With her mother's passing, Irena felt again, and more deeply, the loss of her friends Ewa and Ala to the deportations and the death camps. Rachela, who knows what happened to her? Jadwiga—shot at Pawiak. Żegota and keeping her Jewish children hidden and alive became Irena's only focus. That spring she ran her operations from the apartment safe house of Maria and Henryk Palester. The Nazis continued to draw in their nets and captured a number of Żegota members. At the weekly meetings, more and more, Irena set the agenda and led the decision making.

As spring turned to summer, the underground grapevine reported the Soviet army was approaching Warsaw from the east. The city would soon be a battleground. Occupation forces in the city cracked down with venom on the Polish resistance, which now included a wide swath of Warsaw's population. Germans soldiers went from house to house searching apartments and demanding identity papers. Why they happened to skip by the door of the Palester family, nobody knew.

As the war front marched toward Warsaw, Irena and Janka dug up the lists buried in Jaga's garden, repackaged the entire archive in two glass soda bottles, and under the same apple tree reburied all the names collected since

1939. When Warsaw exploded into street warfare on the first of August, the list held the names of nearly twenty-five hundred Jewish children.

## Final Days in Warsaw

Resistance fighters fell back under German firepower, and to Irena, it seemed a replay of the last days in the ghetto. Wehrmacht and SS soldiers torched buildings block by block, driving people from the basements where they had taken refuge during the battle. As their homes burned, the families were herded into the open squares at gunpoint and mowed down with machine-gun fire.

Irena fled when the Germans arrived in the Mokotov district, where she and her dear Jewish friend, Adam, were hiding with the Palesters. A neighbor, Maria Skokoswska, ran with them. *But where to go?* One thing was certain— they would never report as ordered to the Nazi checkpoint for deportation. They knew what happened to people loaded onto Nazi trains.

Eventually, the group found a hiding place in the ruins of a battered construction site on Lowicka Street and huddled together in the darkness. As Henryk Pales-ter and Maria Skokoswska were both physicians, and Irena and Maria Palester had trained as nurses, the next day they organized an emergency field hospital for wounded resistance fighters and civilians caught up in the turmoil. The hospital quickly became—like anything Irena put her

Irena as a nurse, 1944. *East News Poland*

hand to—a sprawling operation, well organized and efficient, despite the almost complete lack of equipment or medicine.

Adam joined the Palesters' teenage son, Krystof, and two other boys battling the Germans. A few days later, they learned the heartbreaking news Krystof had been killed in the fighting. Making it through the day alive in Mokotov was difficult. Making it through the night was a miracle. No place offered safety. The Nazis turned Warsaw into a killing field. One night Irena stumbled upon a German soldier, and before she could get away, he plunged his bayonet through her leg.

Civil order broke down. It was a challenge to find clean water, and food was running out. At night, Irena lay listening to the quiet breathing of her companions and worried about her hidden children. The stab wound in her leg festered with infection, and the pain kept her from walking far. She struggled to make contact with the foster families. Even in the chaos of the uprising, anti-Semitic blackmailers roamed the streets, threatening denunciations of anyone who might have a bit of change in a pocket.

One day a chance encounter among the rubble revealed an amazing surprise. Irena heard a familiar voice call out, *Over here! Over here!*

She turned, startled, to see a dusty young woman with her blond hair under a cap. The woman waved an arm showing the red badge of the Home Army. *Rachela!*

Irena ran to her friend. Crouching behind the barricades, they embraced, laughing. Irena had counted Rachela among those lost to the *Umschlagplatz*, but here she was, alive, and as beautiful as ever.

Rachela shyly introduced a fair-haired Polish soldier. *My husband.* The man grinned and embraced Irena like an old friend. They had to go their separate ways much too soon, but seeing Rachela bolstered Irena's spirits for some time. Rachela had been like a new women—a soldier, sharp, determined, fighting with a gun in her hand.

With the coming of September, Irena and her friends knew they were losing the fight for Warsaw. German Luftwaffe planes circled over the city on September 9, dropping leaflets. As they fluttered to the streets, people caught them and read their final Nazi warning. Every citizen must leave the city and report to Nazi processing centers. Those who stayed would be executed.

In Mokotov, the friends delayed. Thirty refugees had gathered to hide with them in their makeshift medical clinic, among them two young Jewish children. The *Umschlagplatz* still loomed large in Irena's nightmares. She would not report to any processing center. But two days later, the soldiers arrived, carrying flamethrowers and explosives, intent on burning to the ground every last building. Smoke and dust thickened the air, but did not hide them when the soldiers came upon their crowded basement refuge. Angry and impatient, the

Nazis waved their guns and forced Irena and the others into a convoy marching under guard to the deportation center. Irena struggled to keep up, the bayonet wound to her leg oozing pus. Henryk feared the infection would kill her.

Irena had her mind on protecting a young Jewish child traveling with them, a girl named Anna. She also kept a lookout for an opportunity for the group to escape the death march. Money was the only thing more powerful than a gun. Maybe. It was at least a chance. The friends decided to approach one of the guards and offer a bribe. The German paused a long moment before nodding. *It will be better if you head in that direction, out of the city.* He pointed. *You'll find empty barracks in Okecie. Out by the abandoned airfields.* Placing the roll of bills in an inside pocket, he ambled off in the other direction.

Maria, Malgorzata, and Henryk Palester, along with Dr. Maria Rudolfowa, Irena, Adam, and the girl Anna trekked south leaving Warsaw burning behind them.

## The Warsaw Uprising

By the summer of 1944, German armies east of Poland had been forced into full retreat, suffering heavy losses to the Red Army. On the Western Front, Allied troops had put on the squeeze, landed in France, driving the Germans back toward their homeland. After five brutal years of Nazi occupation, Polish resistance fighters seized the chance to strike back, eager to liberate their capital city. Warsaw could have been one of the first European capitals to wrestle freedom from the Nazis, but Poland was not a matter of great importance to the Allied forces.

Earlier that year, the Polish Home Army had aided the Russians in liberating the cities of Vilnius, Lublin, and Lvov. Now the Red Army amassed just outside Warsaw's eastern suburbs. The Soviets urged the Polish underground to revolt, promising to help them take back Warsaw. Polish leaders did not totally trust the Soviets, but their forces more than doubled the number of German troops in the city, and they were fueled by the desire for freedom. They struck August 1, and within three days took back most of Warsaw. But the Germans wanted Warsaw at all costs. Adolf Hitler had plans to erase Warsaw and on its site build a medieval German town.

The Soviets retreated to nurse their own political plans, which certainly did not include Polish independence. They watched the Home Army and Germans fight it out, refusing to let the Allies—slow to act anyway—use airfields outside the city to provide the Poles food and equipment. Within days, Luftwaffe planes, their underbellies marked with ominous black crosses, swept over the city bombing without mercy. The Polish had no air-defense weapons and to the despair of the city's residents, the battle on the ground turned just as quickly.

From Berlin, German SS Reichsführer Heinrich Himmler

instructed Nazi troops to kill every inhabitant of Warsaw, down to the smallest children. German soldiers went on a rampage, murdering civilians. In two weeks they executed sixty-five thousand people. The German governor of Warsaw, Hans Frank, described the assault: "Almost all Warsaw is a sea of flames. To set houses afire is the surest way to deprive the insurgents out of their hiding places. When we crush the uprising, Warsaw will get what it deserves—complete annihilation."

As their homes burned around them and heavy beams crashed from all directions, the residents driven from their basements were herded into the open squares at gunpoint and mowed down with machine-gun fire. In the words of the "master race," the Polish people were *Untermenschen*—subhumans.

By October it was over. The Warsaw Uprising defeated. The city emptied of all its one million inhabitants. Everything of value had been looted and thirty-three thousand railway wagons filled with furniture, personal belongings, and factory equipment left Warsaw.

German soldiers armed with flamethrowers and explosives systematically demolished house after house. They destroyed churches, schools, hospitals, government and commercial buildings. Museums, the Polish National Archives, and every library went up in flames.

The final death toll stood at 200,000, mostly civilians. Another 150,000 Poles were transported to slave

Members of the Polish underground on a tank they have stolen during the Polish uprising, Summer 1944. *Yad Vashem*

Home Army fighters among rubble during the Warsaw Uprising, 1944. *Yad Vashem*

labor camps in Germany, and 55,000 died in concentration camps that winter. The Soviet and Polish armies at last entered the wasted city on January 17, 1945. By then 80 percent of Warsaw was stone and rubble. A staggering 15 percent of Poland's total prewar population died—6 million people—and is undoubtedly the greatest slaughter perpetrated within a single city in human history. This total includes 90 percent of Poland's Jewish population. At the start of the war, there were an estimated 3.4 million Jews in Poland. Historians say fewer than 11,000 of Warsaw Jews survived.

One of those few who did, Basia Berman, wrote in her diary about what it meant to understand the scale of that destruction: "Even after the final liquidation [of the ghetto], we clung to fairy tales about underground bunkers and sophisticated shelters in which thousands of people are supposedly living. Then we deluded ourselves that they were in the camps and when the nightmare ends will return with a fanfare of victory to the ruins."

But there was a shelter, in which twenty-five thousand Jewish children lived, a secret web stretching through hundreds of hands in Warsaw and across Poland. It was built piece by piece, day by day with bricks of courage and mortar of hope. Of the roughly one million Jewish children in Poland in 1939, about five thousand survived the streets, the ghettos, and the final massacres of the Warsaw Uprising. The number may be low, historians quibble. Double it. Triple it, then. The numbers are still shatteringly small. About half of those were saved by Irena and her network. Irena has been called "the brightest star in the black sky of the occupation."

# 19

## After the War

One warm sunny afternoon, Irena and Janka met in the ruins of Jaga's old back garden, wearing sturdy boots, carrying a large, unwieldy shovel, ready to dig up the names and addresses, the true identities of the Jewish children. In 1945, Warsaw was bleak and treeless. The home had been destroyed in the Warsaw Uprising and since then looted. They found the garden a tangle of twisted metal and brush. They picked among the bricks and rubble, dug and searched for hours, but did not find the treasure they had buried. The lists and Irena's wartime journals and account books, like so much else in the city, were lost forever, destroyed in the destruction and inferno, as the Polish resistance fought to liberate Warsaw.

Irena and her team were undaunted, and set about to recreate large portions of the list from shared memory. Irena admitted there were almost certainly children whose names they had forgotten. The list they reconstructed was punched out on Jaga's old typewriter, salvaged from the ruins. When the names were neatly catalogued, Irena gave the list Dr. Adolf Berman, her colleague in Żegota and postwar head of the Central Committee of Jews in Poland. Adolf Berman ultimately took the list in 1945 to Israel, where the names remain in a sealed archive to respect the privacy of those thousands of families.

In the first weeks after the Soviet liberation, Irena once again encountered **Rachela Rosenthal** by chance on the street. Afterward, that meeting defined something essential for Irena about what it meant to try to piece together a life, as witness and survivor, in the decades that followed.

She and Rachela embraced for a long moment, amidst the wasteland of Warsaw. *We survived hell,* they said to each other, laughing. Then Irena saw that Rachela was crying. She'd never seen Rachela cry before. Irena reached for her friend, and Rachela looked at her sadly. *My name now is Karolina. Only Karolina. Rachela died in the ghetto, Irena. Stanislaw knows nothing of her existence.*

Irena understood, nodded gravely. Part of her had died in the ghetto, too.

Rachela told her she and Stanislaw had a baby—a girl—and they would try to make a future. Dwelling on the past meant reliving intense sorrow. Rachela was a vibrant young woman, and the hardships and deprivations had not destroyed her spirit. She was by nature cheerful

View of the ruins of the Warsaw ghetto. Pictured in the middle are the walls of the Pawiak prison, May 1, 1945. *United States Holocaust Memorial Museum, courtesy of Juliusz Bogdan Deczkowski*

Survivors of the Jewish underground pose after the war atop the ruins of the bunker at number 18 Mila Street, in the former ghetto, July 1, 1945. *United States Holocaust Memorial Museum, courtesy of Leah Hammerstein Silverstein*

and resilient. But like so many in Warsaw, Rachela buried her prewar life completely.

"She never talked about those things again," Irena said later. But, as the women parted on the street, hands touching lightly, Karolina asked, "Sometimes will you remember Rachela?"

*I will,* Irena promised.

Irena threw herself outward. She returned to her job at the city welfare office and dedicated herself to rebuilding them from the ruins. She was quickly appointed director of the citywide welfare services.

**Jaga Piotrowska** and **Jan Dobraczyński** also made their own list of the Jewish children who had passed through the Catholic orphanages during the war and been given new identities, but here, their stories diverged from Irena's.

"When Poland was liberated in 1945, a Jewish community was established," Jaga explains, "and Janek Dobraczyński and I went over to it to give them the lists of the saved children." But Jewish community leaders still remembered those old conversations with Jan Dobraczyński. Dr. Berman quoted Jan's words back to him: *The children themselves would decide their faith when they were old enough.* When the Jewish parents were powerless, Dr. Berman accused, *You baptized the children and made them Christians.*

"During the conversation we were told," Jaga said,

"that we had committed a crime by stealing hundreds of children from the Jewish community, baptizing them, and tearing them away from their Jewish culture. . . . We left completely broken."

Jaga said she treasured "the awareness that I behaved in a decent manner and with dignity." But there was also "a deep wound in my heart." More than fifty Jewish people passed through her home during the years of the occupation, though she risked her life many times over. Forty years later, Jaga's conscience still grappled with these events.

Stanislawa Bussold and her husband, foster parents of baby **Bieta Koppel**, had grown to love her fiercely and adopted the child. They didn't tell Bieta she was Jewish and adopted until after she had grown up. "My birth certificate is a small silver spoon engraved with my name and birth date, a salvaged accessory of a salvaged child," but she honors, too, today the beautiful childhood her foster parents gave her. Bieta has searched for but never found that numbered bank account in Switzerland where the Koppel family fortune may still be waiting.

Ala's daughter, **Rami Gołab-Grynbergowa**, was reunited with her uncle, Sam Gołab, and his wife, Ana, after the war. Like her mother, Rami went on to become both a nurse and a mother. She remains friends today with Elżbieta, the daughter of her wartime protectors, Janusz Strzałecki and Jadwiga Janusz Strzałecka, who helped Irena in her children's network.

Jadwiga Strzałecka with her daughter and three Jewish girls, including Rami Gołab-Grynbergowa, Ala's daughter, 1945.
*Courtesy of the Gołab-Grynbergowa family*

Theodora—the wife of Irena's old friend Jozef, survived life on the Aryan side, and when it was safe, retrieved little **Piotr Zysman** from the orphanage where he had been hidden. Irena never forgot the words of his father when Jozef gave her Piotr to save: *Let him grow up to be a good man and a good Pole*. She had given him the chance, and passed the responsibility back to his mother. **Irka Schultz** survived the war and became a journalist. **Jurek**, real name **Jerzy Korczak**, survived the war, stayed in Poland, and wrote a book about being a boy in the Warsaw ghetto. His romance with Anna Kukulska remained a teenage crush. And the boy named **Jerzy**—whose real name was **Yoram Gross**—went on to be a famous screenwriter in Australia. He died in 2015, but he shared his memories of Irena Sendler for this story.

**Jonas Turkow**, rescued by Nachum and Ala at the *Umschlagplatz,* survived the war and later wrote a testament to Ala's courage, a book with a title that, translated, is *Ala Gołob-Grynberg: The Heroic Nurse of the Warsaw Ghetto.*

Irena continued for decades helping reunite "her" children with their families. "Let me stress most emphatically that we who were rescuing children are not some kind of heroes," Irena insisted to those who wanted to celebrate her actions. "Indeed, that term irritates me greatly. The opposite is true—I continue to have qualms of conscience that I did so little."

· · ·

In a fairy tale or motion picture, this would be the end of Irena Sendler's astonishing biography. We would read that the traumas of the war only touched her lightly. We would read of how her quiet heroism was celebrated across Poland, and that it is only because this happened in a distant country that you have not heard this story.

But after the war, Poland fell from Nazi occupation to Soviet domination. People who had fought for Polish freedom in World War II were considered enemies of the communist state, and throughout the 1940s and 1950s, Irena and her cohorts in the resistance and Żegota were persecuted, targeted, and under constant suspicion.

And so, the story was buried except among the very innermost circle of collaborators and survivors. It was simply too dangerous to speak of what they had done together. Sometimes Irena would still see Rachela—the only one of her Jewish school friends, besides Adam, to survive the ghetto.

"There are times when she avoids me," Irena said of that long postwar friendship. "Sometimes we go two or three years without seeing each other. During those periods she manages to forget the past, at least a little, and enjoy the reality of the present. But sometimes, she's overcome with a longing for her lost loved ones, her parents, her brothers and sisters, and the surroundings in which she grew up. That's when she visits me."

On those days, Irena would be flooded by her own

memories of Ewa and Jozef and Ala and Dr. Korczak and all the lost children. "Of all my most dramatic war-time experiences, including my 'residence' and torture in the Pawiak prison, being tortured by the Gestapo on Szucha Street, watching young people die . . . not one left so great an impression on me as the sight of Korczak and his children marching to their death," Irena said. And, in her sleep, even decades after the war, Irena was haunted by nightmares about those who perished. "In my dreams," Irena said, "I still hear the cries when they were leaving their parents."

While it was impossible to speak of Irena's stories in communist Poland, in Israel, the United States, and Canada, many of the infants and toddlers whom Irena and her network of friends had helped save were growing up. By the mid-1960s the youngest of them were in their twenties. In the west, Irena's children started telling the stories.

In 1965, based on that burgeoning body of testimony—and especially on the wartime testimony of Jonas Turkow—Yad Vashem, the Holocaust memorial organization in Israel, awarded Irena its highest honor. Irena Sendler was named to the list of Righteous Among the Nations, and in her honor an olive tree was planted on the Mount of Remembrance. According to Jewish tradition, there are in every generation a small number of people whose goodness renovates the entire world in the face of evil, and Irena was named among them. So, too, in time were

Jaga Piotrowska, Maria Kukulska, Irka Schultz, Maria Palester, Jadwiga Deneka, Wladyslawa Marynowska, Janka Grabowska, Julian and Halina Grobelny, and even Jan Dobraczyński.

The Soviets, however, refused to authorize Irena's passport so she could travel to Jerusalem to accept the award. Irena had been branded a decadent western dissident and a public menace.

So the story again faded from memory. By the late 1970s, many of those who had survived the war were passing on. One day in 1979, Irena and Jaga met with two women in their old network, and they jointly authored a statement recording the story of their collaboration for history. That statement reads, "We estimate (today after forty years it is difficult to determine it exactly) the number of children which Żegota helped in various ways to be around 2,500."

Irena was always emphatic that she did not save them alone. "Every time people said that she saved 2,500 Jewish children's lives," Yoram Gross—the wartime boy known as Jerzy—recalls, "she corrected this by saying that she doesn't know the exact number and that she was saving the children together with friends that helped her." And, as Irena said late in life, "I want everyone to know that, while I was coordinating our efforts, we were about twenty to twenty five people. I did not do it alone."

After the war, when Irena made a list of all the people

who at one moment or another did something to help her network in Warsaw to help Jewish families and save their children, it was fourteen pages long, and the names numbered in the dozens upon dozens. What Irena always believed was that she was one member of a vast collective effort of decency. That's how she wanted the world to remember her.

Also in 1979, an international conference was held on Holocaust rescuers and their stories. There, Professor Ina Friedman spoke, saying, he believed eventually hundreds of inspiring stories would come to light in Poland. "If we knew," he told the crowd that day, "the names of all the noble people who risked their lives to save the Jews, the area around Yad Vashem would be full of trees and would turn into a forest."

But it was not until the beginning of Glasnost in the late 1980s, when Irena, in her seventies, was allowed to travel to Israel and meet again, face to face, with many of the children whose lives she saved. Scenes of that reunion were inspiring, and heartbreaking. These children only knew her—if they knew her at all as toddlers or infants— as Jolanta, the last face of their childhood.

When the Cold War ended in the 1990s, Irena's story was finally told in Poland. Her heroism was discovered by a group of American high school students, looking for a topic for their history project. Their work, chronicled in a memoir, *Life in a Jar*, brought Irena to the attention of the mainstream media. By the turn of the millennium, people around the world celebrated the story, celebrated such courage, compassion, and self-sacrifice in the face of overwhelming evil. But now Irena, in her nineties, was one of the few living survivors of her network, and parts of the truth were already lost to history. "I only have recourse to the memories burned into my mind by the events of those days," Irena said.

In 2008, at the age of ninety-eight, having borne witness not just to the better part of a century but also to the lives of thousands who survived because of her courage, Irena Sendler died peacefully in Warsaw, surrounded by several of "her" children. She is buried in a wooded cemetery in Warsaw, and perhaps it is a mark of her fame now that many days the simple tombstone is alight with candles and awash with small bouquets of flowers brought by friends and strangers. There, in the calm of a Polish forest, the flame of her memory is not a blaze, but there is often a quiet light in shadows. On her gravestone are only the dates of her life and the names of her parents. But if we could add a more elaborate epitaph, perhaps we would engrave the words of Mahatma Gandhi: "A small body of determined spirits fired by an unquenchable faith in their mission can alter the course of history." Irena, her friends and collaborators proved these words true.

*Irena Sendler*
2007, East News Poland

# Adapter's Note

In adapting this story from the book by Tilar Mazzeo, I have followed her lead in constructing a narrative based on the archives and historical sources. In several instances, I have given insight into a character's thoughts or feelings or offered reframed dialogue. Where material is presented in italics, or in some cases where I describe a character's interior thoughts or feelings, the details are not directly present in the historical record. However, following in the spirit of Tilar Mazzeo's book, these "fly-on-the-wall" moments are not without historical basis or a factual scaffolding based in research. Sometimes, these moments are based on Irena's recollections of her friends, where she records only one side of the conversation. The material in italics fills in the logical gap and provides the substance of the other side of that conversation for the reader. Other times, the insights into Irena's private experience or the experience of her friends are based on an overall picture of the evidence that they or others left behind about what it was like to live through the events in this story. It is also based on Tilar Mazzeo's knowledge, from extensive research and personal interviews, of who they were as people and how they are most likely to have acted or reacted. In writing from an individual character's perspective to describe what he or she would have seen and experienced, especially in scenes narrating events and places in Warsaw, I have sometimes relied on historical photographs, other eyewitness accounts of an event, and maps, as well as the book by Tilar Mazzeo. Reconstructed monologue or dialogue appears in italics in the book; direct dialogue or testimony appears in quotations. I have used my best judgment in trying to portray Irena's story as truthfully as possible, while acknowledging the possibility of error in attempting to reveal historical events without the benefit of complete records and the difficulty of filling in the gaps in narrating the experiences of other people. The sources are, in each case, noted. I have in a few instances modified past-tense eyewitness testimony to the present tense, in order to tell the story as these people experienced it.

## ADAPTER ACKNOWLEDGMENTS

I would like to express my great appreciation to senior editor Ruta Rimas and author Tilar J. Mazzeo for allowing me to have a hand in sharing the story of Irena Sendler, her network, and the Jewish people of Warsaw. I am truly humbled and honored to have the chance to bring this story to young readers. I would also like to thank my long-time friend and nonfiction writer Claire Rudolf Murphy for reading chapters and offering counsel. As ever, I'm grateful to Mike for his endless support and love.

# Endnotes

### Prologue

**p. 4:** "Be quiet... must not cry.": IPNTV, "Relacja Piotra Zettingera o ucieczce z warszawskiego getta" [video interview of Piotr Zettinger], YouTube video, 13:27, posted April 19, 2013, https://www.youtube.com/watch?v=tY3WxXUiYzo.

### Chapter 1

**p. 7:** "faraway surf . . . not a calm surf but when waves crash onto a beach": Diane Ackerman, *The Zookeeper's Wife: A War Story*, New York: W. W. Norton, 2008, 32.

### Chapter 2

**p. 22:** "families where one herring was shared amongst six children . . .": Magdelena Grochowska, "Lista Sendlerowj." "Reportaž Z 2001 Roku," *Gazeta Wyborcza,* May 12, 2008, n.p.

### Chapter 3

**p. 27:** "So we forged . . .": "Irena Sendler," Museum of the History of Polish Jews, http://www.sprawiedliwi.org.pl/en/cms/biography-83/.

## Chapter 4

**p. 37**: "Recently Jews who left . . . merciless severity.": Gunnar S. Paulsson, *Secret City: The Hidden Jews of Warsaw 1940–1945*, New Haven: Yale University Press, 2002, 67.

**p. 42**: "The Jews will die . . . Jewish question.": State University of New York at Buffalo / Jagiellonian University, "Slow Extermination: Life and Death in the Warsaw Ghetto," *Info Poland*, http ://info-poland.buffalo.edu/web/history/WWII/ghetto/slow.html.

## Chapter 5

**p. 44**: "The first time I went into the ghetto . . . covered with a newspaper.": "Irena Sendler," [video interview with Irena Sendler] YouTube video, 0:05, posted April 25, 2010, https://youtu.be /dvycQNINaKg.

**p. 46**: "Who should get the vaccinations?": Sendler, "Youth Associations of the Warsaw Ghetto: A Tribute to Jewish Rescuers," ZIH archives (Materialy Zabrane w Latach, 1995–2003, szgn. S/353). Trans. Stanislaw Barańczak and Michael Barańczak.

**p. 49**: "Abuses—wild, bestial 'amusements'—are daily events": Władysław Bartoszewski, *The Warsaw Ghetto: A Christian's Testimony.* Trans. Stephen G. Cappellari. Boston: Beacon Press, 1987.

**p. 49**: "Most nations would weep . . . soldiers laugh.": Irene Tomaszewski and Tecia Werbowski, *Code Name: Żegota: Rescuing Jews in Occupied Poland, 1942–1945: The Most Dangerous Conspiracy in Wartime Europe,* Oxford, England: Praeger, May 2010, 13.

**p. 50**: "A child smuggler caught by a German . . . to be amputated.": Irene Tomaszewski and Tecia Werbowski, *Code Name: Żegota*, 15.

**p. 50**: A Jewish child said, "I would like to be a dog and I wouldn't be afraid that they would kill me.": Ibid.

**p. 55**: "Don't you people understand yet? . . . There is no crying allowed here!": Sendler, "Youth Associations of the Warsaw Ghetto."

**p. 58**: "In a darkened room . . . closed it.": Irene Tomaszewski and Tecia Werbowski, *Code Name: Żegota*, 15.

## Chapter 6

**p. 60–62:** "For an absurdly low salary . . . work day.": Mirosława Pałaszewska, private communications with Tilar J. Mazzeo.

**p. 63:** "Why are you standing? . . . Because I am Polish.": Ed. Robert Blobaum, *Anti-Semitism and Its Opponents in Modern Poland*, Ithaca: Cornell University Press, 2005; also Grochowska, "Lista Sendlerowj."

**p. 69:** "You have to stand up . . . give a hand.": Variations of this quote appear in a number of sources quoting interviews given by Irena Sendler in the years before she died.

**p. 72:** "A few minutes before curfew . . . young beggers.": Jan Engelgard, "To Dobraczyński był bohaterem tamtego czasu." *Konserwatyzm,* June 19, 2013, http://www.konserwatyzm.pl /artykul/10342/to-dobraczynski-byl-bohaterem-tamtego-czasu.

**p. 73–74:** "Above the entrance . . . one rung to another.": *The Last Eyewitnesses: Children of the Holocaust Speak.* Ed. Jakub Gutembaum and Agnieszka Lałała. Vol. 2. Evanston, IL: Northwestern University Press, 2005.

**p. 77:** "Please don't ask me," she told Irena: Irena Sendler, "Youth Associations of the Warsaw Ghetto."

## Chapter 7

**p. 81:** "You can be calm.": "Irena Schultz," Polish Righteous [Among Nations], database.

**p. 84:** "It was enough to know . . .": Andrezj Marynowski, personal communication.

## Chapter 8

**p. 91:** "It looked like . . .": Jon E. Lewis, *Voices from the Holocaust.* https://books.google.com/books?id=fE7BBAAAQBAJ&pg=PT7 1&dq=It+looked+like+a+normal+large+lorry,+in+grey+paint,&h l=en&sa=X&ved=0ahUKEwizm_HuqJPKAhUW9mMKHZF2 DHYQ6AEIMDAA#v=onepage&q=It%20looked%20like%20

a%20normal%20large%20lorry%2C%20in%20grey%20
paint%2C&f=false.

## Chapter 9

**p. 104:** It is a difficult thing," he wrote, "to be born and to learn to live": Janusz Korczak, *Ghetto Diary*, New Haven: Yale University Press, 2003.

**p. 118:** "Make sure he grows up to be a good Pole and an honorable man.": Tilar J. Mazzeo, *Irena's Children*, New York: Simon & Schuster, 2016.

**p. 121:** "The SS men . . . said it was to be a bath.": Chris Webb and Michal Chocholatý, *The Treblinka Death Camp: History, Biographies, Remembrance*, Stuttgart: ibidem Press, 2014, 14, 21, passim.

## Chapter 10

**p. 124:** "You do not leave a sick child in the night": Diane Ackerman, *The Zookeeper's Wife*.

**p. 125:** "I cannot leave the children even for a moment": Stanislaw Adler, *In the Warsaw Ghetto: 1940–1943, An Account of a Witness: The Memoirs of Stanislaw Adler*. Trans. Sara Philip. Jerusalem: Yad Vashem, 1982, p 90.

**p. 126:** "I used my last ounce . . . call a doctor": "Irena Sendler Tells the Story of Janusz Korczak," GARIWO; http://lewicowo .pl/o-pomocy-zydom/.

**p. 128:** "I give my child in your care, raise my child as if it was yours": "Ala Gołąb-Grynberg," Warsaw Ghetto Database, Polish Center for Holocaust Research, http://warszawa.getto.pl/index. php?mod=view_record&rid=07051998094230000004&tid=oso by&lang=en.

**p. 128:** "mother, father, sister . . . biggest consolation.": Irena Sendler, "Youth Associations of the Warsaw Ghetto."

**p. 132:** "quiet, soothing, and full of kindness.": Ibid.

**p. 133:** "the only way to save the children was to get them out.": "Irena Sendler Tells the Story of Janusz Korczak," GARIWO.

### Chapter 11

**p. 135:** "The trains, already leaving . . . hold them all.": Władysław Bartoszweski, *The Warsaw Ghetto*. See also Abraham Lewin, *A Cup of Tears: A Diary of the Warsaw Ghetto*, ed. Antony Polonsky, Waukegan, IL: Fontana Press, 1990; see entries for July 1942.

**p. 138:** "If more than 300,000 Jews are to be annihilated . . . the entire community." Nahum Bogner, "The Convent Children: The Rescue of Jewish Children in Polish Convents During the Holocaust," Shoah Resource Center, Yad Vashem, p.7 www.yadvashem .org/yv/en/righteous/pdf/resources/nachum_bogner.pdf.

### Chapter 12

**p. 151:** "Well, Jolanta, we're striking a good deal . . . people.": Marcin Mierzejewski, "Sendler's Children," *Warsaw Voice*, September 25, 2003, www.warsawvoice.pl/WVpage/pages/articlePrint .php/3568/article

**p. 155–156:** *Please, help me. . . .* "The tram is broken, I'm returning to the depot.": News clippings, undated, "Jaga Piotrowska" and "Stowarzszenie Dzieci Holocaustu W Polsce," courtesy Association of the Children of the Holocaust in Poland, archives; private correspondence with the author. See also "50 Razy Kara Śmierci: Z Jadwigą Piotrowską," May 11, 1986, ZIH, Materialy Zabrane w Latach, 1995–2003, szgn. S/353.

### Chapter 13

**p. 163:** *How dare you foul bandits attack the peace of a Polish Christian:* "Irena Sendlerowa, O Pomocy Żydom," *Lewicowo.pl*, October 6, 2011, http://lewicowo.pl/o-pomocy-zydom/.

**p. 174:** "So now we are just like the others?": News clippings courtesy private archives of Mirosława Pałaszewska; private communications with Tilar J. Mazzeo.

## Chapter 14

p. 179–180: "Give me some addresses where we can take people who make it to the Aryan side": Teresa Prekerowa, *Żegota: Commission d'aide aux Juifs,* Trans. Maria Apfelbaum, Monaco: Rocher, 1999.

p. 180: "'emergency rooms' . . . ghetto could show up.": Ibid.

p. 183: "There was no air, only black, choking smoke. . . . under our feet.": Marek Edelman, "The Ghetto Fights," *The Warsaw Ghetto: The 45th Anniversary of the Uprising,* Interpress Publishers, http://www.writing.upenn.edu/~afilreis/Holocaust/warsaw-uprising .html.

p. 186: "Jews, bandits, and subhumans were destroyed. The Jewish Quarter of Warsaw is no more.": Marian Apfelbaum, *Two Flags: Return to the Warsaw Ghetto,* New York: Gefen Publishing, 2007, 317.

p. 186: "half-walked, half-crawled for twenty hours": "Marek Edelman: Last Surviving Leader of the 1943 Warsaw Ghetto Uprising Against the Nazis," *The Independent*, October 7, 2009, obituary.

## Chapter 15

p. 189: "It's the lists of children. . . . Hide it.": "Irena Sendlerowa," Museum of the History of Polish Jews, http://www.sprawiedliwi .org.pl/pl/cms/biografia-83/.

p. 198: "Don't spoil her, Stasiu . . . what her life will be like.": Magdelena Grochowska, "Lista Sendlerowj." "Reportaž Z 2001 Roku," *Gazeta Wyborcza,* May 12, 2008, n.p.

## Chapter 16

p. 202: "We are doing everything we can to get you out of that hell": Irene Tomaszewski and Tecia Werbowski, *Code Name: Żegota.*

p. 209: *Be strong. We love you.*: Ibid.

**Chapter 17**

p. 211: "You are free. Save yourself fast.": Teresa Prekerowa, *Żegota: Commission d'aide aux Juifs*. And autobiography.

p. 212: "You lousy thug, get lost.": Irena Sendler, autobiographical notes, ZIH archives, Materialy Zabrane w Latach, 1995–2003, szgn. S/353, file IS-04-85-R.

p. 214: "They were looking for you again": Ibid.

**Chapter 18**

p. 219–220: "Which is the dead woman's daughter?": "Irena Sendlerowa," Association of the Children of the Holocaust in Poland, www.dzieciholocaustu.org.pl/szab58.php?s=en_sendlerowa.php.

p. 227: "Almost all Warsaw is a sea of flames. . . . annihilation.": Adolf Ciborowski, *Warsaw, a City Destroyed and Rebuilt*, Interpress Publishers, Warsaw, 1969. p. 48.

p. 229: "Even after the final liquidation [of the ghetto], we clung to fairy tales about underground bunkers": Ada Pagis, "A Rare Gem," *Haaretz,* May 9, 2008, http://www.haaretz.com/a-rare-gem-1.245497; review of *Ir betoch ir* [City Within a City], diary of Batia Temkin-Berman, trans. Uri Orlev, Jerusalem: Yad Vashem, 2008.

p. 230: The brightest star in the black sky of the occupation": Iwona Rojek, "To była matka całego świata—corka Ireny Sendler opowiedziała nam o swojej mamie," *Echo DniaSiłętokrzyskie*, December 9, 2012, www.echodnia.eu/swietokrzyskie/wiadom osci/kielce/art/8561374,to-byla-matka-calego-swiata-corka-ireny-sendler-opowiedziala-nam-o-swojej-mamie,id,t.html.

**Chapter 19**

p. 234: "She never talked about those things again.": Irena Sendler, "Youth Associations of the Warsaw Ghetto."

p. 234: "When Poland was liberated in 1945 . . . saved children.":

Archives of Mirosława Pałaszewska and personal correspondence; also Michal Głowiński, *The Black Seasons*, 87.

**p. 234–235:** "During the conversation . . . a deep wound in my heart.": Ibid.

**p. 235:** "My birth certificate is a small silver spoon engraved with my name and birth date": "Elżbieta Ficowska," testimony, Association of the Children of the Holocaust in Poland, http://www.dzieciholocaustu.org.pl/szab58.php?s=en_myionas_11.php.

**p. 237:** "Let me stress most emphatically that we who were rescuing children are not some kind of heroes": "Irena Sendlerowa," Association of the Children of the Holocaust in Poland.

**p. 238:** "There are times when she avoids me. . . . That's when she visits me.": Irena Sendler, "Youth Associations of the Warsaw Ghetto."

**p. 239:** "Of all my most dramatic war-time experiences, including my 'residence' and torture in the Pawiak": Janusz Korczak, "A Child's Right to Respect." Strasbourg: Council of Europe Publishing, 2009, http://www.coe.int/t/commissioner/source/prems/PublicationKorczak_en.pdf.

**p. 239:** "In my dreams," Irena said, "I still hear the cries": Joseph Bottum, "Good People, Evil Times: The Women of Żegota," *First Things,* 2009, http://www.firstthings.com/blogs/firstthoughts/2009/04/good-people-evil-times-the-women-of-zegota.

**p. 240:** "We estimate (today after 40 years it is difficult to determine it exactly) the number of children which Żegota helped in various ways to be around 2,500.": Tilar J. Mazzeo, *Irena's Children*, New York: Simon & Schuster, 2016.

**p. 240:** "Every time people . . . helped her.": Yoram Gross conversation with Tilar J. Mazzeo.

**p. 240:** "I want everyone to know that, while I was coordinating our efforts, we were about twenty": Joachim Wieler, "The Long Path to Irena Sendler: Mother of the Holocaust Children," [interview with Irena Sendler], *Social Work and Society: International*

*Online Journal*, vol. 4, no. 1 (2006), http://www.socwork.net/sws /article/view/185/591.

**p. 241:** "If we knew . . . would turn into a forest.": Hans G. Furth, "One million Polish rescuers of hunted Jews?," *Journal of Genocide Research*, 1:2 (1999): 227–232.

**p. 242:** "I only have recourse . . . of those days": Irena Sendler, auto-biographical notes, ZIH archives, Materialy Zabrane w Latach, 1995–2003, szgn. S/353, file IS-04-85-R.

**p. 242:** "A small body of determined spirits fired by an unquench-able faith in their mission can alter the course of history.": Anil Dutta Mishra, *Inspiring Thoughts of Mahatma Gandhi*, Delhi: Concept Publishing, 2008, 36.

# READING GROUP GUIDE

*Irena's Children: Young Readers Edition*
by Tilar J. Mazzeo,
adapted by Mary Cronk Farrell

## Discussion Questions

1. As the author asks in the introduction, referring to Irena: "If you had been alive during the dark days of the Second World War, would you have been one of the people who joined her?" Why or why not? Do you think that Irena and her friends were just "brave and average" or was there something special about them?

2. Name some of the different ways that people in the book participated in resistance acts. What kind of resistance work would you have been likely to participate in? Could you have been one of the teen assassins? A member of the underground press?

3. Why did Irena's story take so long to be told? Why is it important to understand and celebrate the "average" people who take action during dark times in history? Can

you think of other citizen activists, historical or contemporary? Do you think there are many others whose stories have been quietly buried?

4. Throughout history, people have commonly blamed others for bad things that happen, which often resulted in discrimination, violence, and sometimes genocide. How does the history of the Jewish people reflect this? What new information did you learn about Jewish culture from reading this book? Are there groups of people who currently experience hate and discrimination, like Jews did during the time of the Holocaust?

5. Were some of the acts committed by the Nazis that were described in the book difficult to read about? Which ones? Do you think that every single Nazi was evil? Why did the author choose not to portray any sympathetic Nazis? Does it help, as the author says, to recognize Irena's bravery by comparing it to the Nazis' brutality?

6. Discuss how Irena's job as a social worker meant that she might be more open to helping the Jews in the Warsaw ghetto. Provide examples from the book of how her position enabled her to smuggle children out to safety.

7. After the invasion, why did the Nazis choose to immediately round up and kill teachers, priests, politicians,

journalists, and other community leaders? What evidence does the book provide as to why they chose to close schools and burn down libraries? Why do you think they believed that reading, writing, thinking, and teaching were dangerous?

8. Not all of the Polish people were sympathetic to the Jews. Give examples of some ways in which they betrayed the Jews, either out of anti-Semitism or to save themselves.

9. When the Jews were first moved into the ghetto, many of them felt they would be safer there. Why did they think that? Why did some others, like Maria Palester and Vera Gran, decide to "hide in the open" and remain friendly with some Germans throughout the occupation? Do you see them as determined survivors or sellouts? What do you think their neighbors and friends thought of them?

10. From almost the moment that the ghetto walls were erected, people began escaping from it. Name some of the ways they escaped. Would you have tried to escape? How would you have done it?

11. Discuss some of the money issues during this time. Was it true that bribes could "solve all sorts of problems"? Did the fact that some rich Jews were "ghetto aristocrats" and lived in the "better" parts of the ghetto make things

easier for them? How did Irena's efforts increase after she was given funding by the official resistance? Why do you think people are more willing to do things for money that they would not otherwise do?

12. Name some of the different ways that parents tried to send their children out of the ghetto, to safety. Why is it that parents were willing to be parted from their children to make them safe? Discuss how this transpires in modern-day America, with the arrival of Mexican and Central American children unaccompanied by their parents.

13. Name some of the immoral or dishonest things that Irena and others did in order to save the children. Is it ever right to do the wrong thing, in your opinion?

14. In April 1943, ghetto residents decided to strike back, attacking with bombs and guns. Why do you think it took so long for an uprising to occur? Might they have been successful if they had tried this when their numbers were greater? In your opinion, is it better to fight in the open than to work in secret as Irena and her friends did?

15. Discuss this statement from the book: "the war made all sorts of decent people fainthearted." How can friendships be beneficial, but also perilous, in times of war? Was

Irena ever betrayed by any of her friends? How would you know whether to trust your friends or not?

16. Have you read other books about the Holocaust or seen movies or TV shows about this period in history? Were they true stories or fiction? How did the tone of this book compare with other depictions?

17. What is your impression of Irena Sendler? Are you surprised by her bravery? How do you think she will be remembered in Jewish history?

*Guide prepared in 2016 by Bobbie Combs, a consultant at We Love Children's Books*

*A full curriculum guide written in alignment to the Common Core standards is posted on simonandschuster.net.*

Make this a family reading experience
with the original edition of
*Irena's Children* by Tilar J. Mazzeo

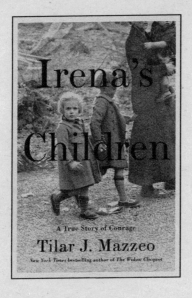

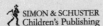

**W**ant to know what dogs are thinking?
What they feel, and what they can smell
with that great big nose of theirs?
This book, by dog owner and scientist
Alexandra Horowitz, is as close as you can get to
knowing about dogs without *being* a dog yourself.

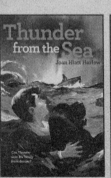